D1457655

SO-BLB-735

NEW ENGLAND
WILDFLOWERS

A Guide to Common Plants

FRANK KACZMAREK

FALCONGUIDES ®

GUILFORD, CONNECTICUT
HELENA, MONTANA

AN IMPRINT OF THE GLOBE PEQUOT PRESS

FALCONGUIDES®

Copyright © 2009 by Morris Book Publishing, LLC

Text design: Nancy Freeborn
Map © Morris Book Publishing, LLC
All photographs by Frank Kaczmarek unless otherwise indicated.

Library of Congress Cataloging-in-Publication Data
Kaczmarek, Frank S.
  New England wildflowers : a guide to common plants / Frank Kaczmarek.
      p. cm. — (Falcon guide)
   ISBN 978-0-7627-4820-4
  1. Wild flowers—New England—Handbooks, manuals, etc. I. Title. II. Series.

QK121.K33 2009
582.130974—dc22

                                                    2008031370

Printed in China
10 9 8 7 6 5 4 3 2 1

TO EK AND PR

In Loving Memory

CONTENTS

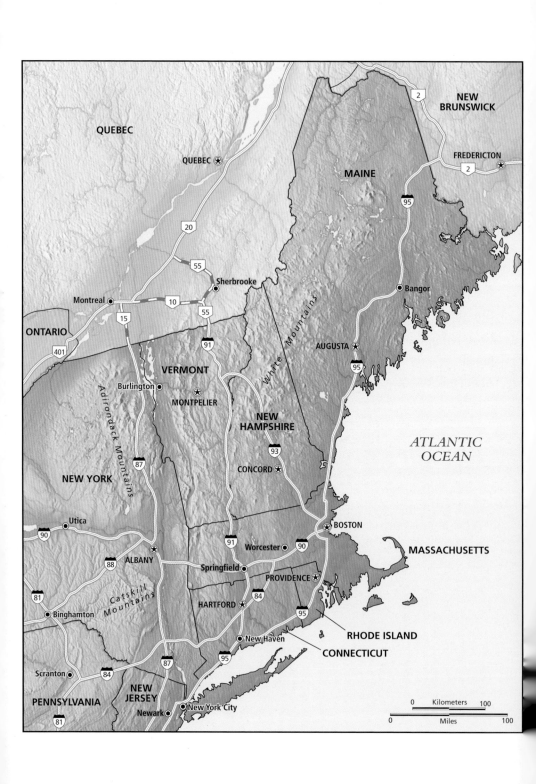

ACKNOWLEDGMENTS

Many thanks to Carole Drong, graphic artist and photographer, for all her help; and to photographer Henry Wolcott for providing an image of Featherfoil, when I failed to locate the species. Thanks, also, to Jeff Sims, fellow naturalist and photographer, for providing the photograph of the author and for numerous helpful discussions on the nature of New England. I would also like to thank all the staff at Globe Pequot who had a hand in making this field guide a reality, especially to Erin Turner, who gave me the chance to share a small part of the New England that I love, as well as Leah Gilman and John Burbidge, who guided me through the editorial process. Special thanks go to my wife and best friend, Colleen, for tolerating my many absences while working on the book and being a constant companion on my forays into the "north country."

INTRODUCTION

The states of Connecticut, Rhode Island, Massachusetts, Vermont, New Hampshire, and Maine make up the area known as New England. The region, located in the northeastern corner of the continental United States, covers an area of approximately 70,000 square miles, roughly equal in size to the state of Missouri.

About New England and Its Flora

Prehistory

New England formed several hundred million years ago: a result of North America colliding with western Africa. The last several million years saw the region's landscape repeatedly scoured by glaciers. Known as the Laurentide Ice Sheet, the last glacier to cover New England occurred roughly 20,000 years ago and blanketed much of the region in ice up to a mile thick. Around 12,000 years ago the earth's climate began to warm slowly, melting the glacial ice pack and leaving New England with a tundralike environment similar to that found in northern Canada today. Cold-tolerant flora, such as sedges, birches, willows, and spruce, were the pioneer species to populate this new habitat. The milder climate, which persisted for about 1,000 years, paved the way for additional tree species—evergreens such as pine, larch, and fir—to make their way into the region. Over time forests composed mainly of evergreens and a few hardwoods such as oak and ash dominated much of the New England landscape. After a relatively short period of time geologically speaking, the warming trend abated. The return to a cooler climate pattern forced the forest composition back to one dominated by cold-tolerant species. Oak and ash disappeared completely from the forest makeup. At the same time, based on archeological evidence, the first humans were believed to have migrated into the region. The cooler climate persisted for about 800–1,000 years. Then roughly 10,000 years ago, New England once again returned to a warmer climate pattern and, within a scant 1,000 years, a fairly well-developed hardwood forest spread into the region. Forests once again covered a significant portion of New England.

The Changing New England Landscape

Since the arrival of the first European settlers some 400 years ago, the landscape of New England has undergone profound changes. Forests were more extensive in pre-colonial New England. Large areas of forest surrounding Native American settlements (particularly those along the coast) had a much more open feel to them and were park-like in appearance. These areas had little underbrush as the native peoples regularly set fires as a means of controlling its growth. This made travel and hunting less difficult and also facilitated the gathering of nuts and berries. It was also an effective strategy for reducing pest insect populations (such as fleas and ticks) and in keeping the lands used for planting crops open. Europeans began to settle into the region in the early 1600s. They saw the forests of North America as a commodity that would not only provide land for agriculture but would provide material that could be sent back to European markets, which were starved for timber. When the first English colonists arrived in North America, they had left behind a country that was, at best, 10 percent forested. Once begun, the intense level of deforestation significantly transformed the ecology of the region that is now known as New England.

The colonists quickly cleared large tracts of forest. Initially, the driving force was to create land for agricultural use. As the immigrant population continued to grow, additional forestlands were cleared to satisfy an ever-increasing need for more farmland as well as new grazing land to accommodate the burgeoning livestock populations. The colonists also saw in these forests a virtually unlimited storehouse of timber to supply their building and energy needs. Fences were an integral part of any farm. The colonists preferred wooden fences to stone walls. Stone walls, which many have come to think of as a quintessential element of the New England landscape, were used only after the favored lumber for fence building became too scarce and expensive for the average farmer to continue using. Timber also supplied the primary source of energy to heat homes and for cooking fuel. A typical colonial household might burn as much as 30 to 40 cords of wood a year in this endeavor.

The relentless pace of deforestation had serious environmental consequences for the land. The physical characteristics of these heavily deforested areas changed rapidly. The soil warmed up earlier in the season and was prone to dry out much quicker. This

Rocky outcrop

3

Old field with grasses and trees

resulted in the land becoming warmer in summer and colder in the winter than the surrounding forests. This new open landscape was highly susceptible to wind erosion and to increased flooding. As a consequence soil nutrients were more rapidly depleted. The land quickly lost its ability to sustain agriculture, and this in turn fed the need to clear more land for agriculture and livestock.

Grazing land brought about additional problems. Native grasses such as wild rye and broom straw were considered substandard in nutritional quality to serve as livestock feed. To overcome this problem, many plant species, such as Orchard Grass and White Clover, favored in Europe, were introduced into the region. Lacking natural control factors, many of these nonnative varieties quickly adapted to their new environment, often at the expense of native species. Over time many species considered weeds also became established. Examples include chickweeds, burdock, dandelion, chicory, and plantains. By the early 1700s additional species such as Red Clover, Timothy Grass, and Alfalfa were introduced as additional livestock feed. Native grasses like the bluestems continued to lose ground.

Northern hardwood forest

As the land continued to be cleared, vegetables and grains, along with orchard trees, became the dominant flora in the landscape.

Forestlands continued to be converted to pastureland at a frenzied pace. By 1800 the amount of forestland still exceeded the amount of cleared land but by the smallest percentage. New England had become a pastoral setting. In addition to the loss of significant tracts of forestlands, the composition of the remaining forest had shifted dramatically. By the mid-1800s, Connecticut, Rhode Island, and Massachusetts had lost 75 percent or more of their forested lands. Vermont, New Hampshire, and Maine saw a smaller percentage loss largely because topography and climate made access to these forests more difficult. During the later 1800s a substantial number of farmers abandoned their lands in New England for the promise of the rich prairies of the Midwest. Slowly forests began to replace pastureland. However, the clear-cutting of the forests by logging companies continued unabated in an effort to supply a rapidly industrializing nation with an unending need for lumber. Today 60 to 80 percent of New England is once again forested. However, suburban

sprawl and a growing human population threaten to continue fragmenting and shrinking the existing forestlands.

Major Forest Communities Today

The temperate forests of New England are world famous for their spectacular fall foliage. New England is composed of several forest communities. An oak-hickory forest prevails in the southern portion of the region that covers Connecticut, Rhode Island, and eastern Massachusetts. The dominant tree species include the oaks (red, black, and white), hickory, hemlock, and scattered stands of white pine. Pine-oak forest is found in southeastern Massachusetts and Cape Cod and in north-central Rhode Island. These poor-quality soils are home to Pitch Pine and a number of oak species. The northern hardwood forest can be found throughout Vermont, the upper two-thirds of New Hampshire, and most of Maine. Here beeches, birches, maples, red spruce, hemlock, balsam fir, and red and white pines characterize the forests. A transition zone containing a mix of oak-hickory and northern hardwood forest communities can be found throughout western Massachusetts and southern New Hampshire and along the Connecticut River north of Springfield, Massachusetts. Also, scattered in areas of northern Maine and in the mountains of Vermont and New Hampshire are the boreal (spruce-fir) forests (which are not covered in this book).

Nearly 13 percent of the land surface of New England is covered with fresh water. New England has numerous rivers, lakes, ponds, and streams. In addition, all types of wetland habitats from marshes to bogs to wet meadows can be found in all the New England states.

Open areas are also widespread throughout the region and are created by natural or man-made disturbances and include such habitats as fields and meadows.

Invasive Species

It is estimated that since the arrival of the first Europeans, some 50,000 plant species have been introduced into North America either deliberately or by accident, and New England was an early staging area. The colonists saw native species as alien and somewhat forbidding and wanted to surround themselves with the more familiar varieties of home; so they introduced a number of plant (and animal) species for use as food, medicine, and landscaping. Many of the major food crops we grow today are introduced species. The colonists

Invasive Yellow Flag Iris in wetlands

7

Whitetail fawn

were responsible for the first wave of invasive species into North America. Today, globalization and climate change continue to fuel the problem.

Twenty-five percent of all the vascular plant species found in the United States today are alien species. Some introduced species naturalize (the wildflower Ragged Robin is an example) while others can spread unchecked, causing potentially serious environmental problems such as is seen with Purple Loosestrife. There is an economic toll as well. Invasive species, some experts estimate, currently cause in the neighborhood of $20 billion a year in damages in the United States alone, and that figure is expected to continue rising.

In addition to habitat loss and climate change, invasive species can contribute to species extinction. Currently more than 3,000 species of plants and animals become extinct around the world every year, and the yearly numbers are increasing. At the current rate it is estimated that by the year 2100 half of the known species on earth will become extinct. If this is allowed to happen, the earth will indeed be a less interesting and poorer place.

How to Use This Book

This guide contains the photographs and descriptions of more than 350 species of wild-flowers, common flowering shrubs, grasses, sedges, and rushes that are found in New England. The majority of species described are native to the region; that is, they were present in the landscape before the arrival of the first colonists. A number of introduced species are also included in the book and comprise roughly 20 percent of the total described. It is the author's belief that it is as important to recognize introduced species as it is to recognize native species and to understand the subtle and occasionally significant impact nonnative species have on the environment. Species endemic to specialized habitats such as the Atlantic coast or alpine regions (areas over 3,000 feet above sea level) are not included in this book. Initially the plants are broadly divided into sections based on flower color. The species description is then arranged alphabetically by family name. This groups related members of the same family together.

Flower Color

In this as in most wildflower field guides the first characteristic used to begin the identification process is flower color. While the use of flower color is a simple and obvious first step, it is far from perfect. Flowers can be variable with respect to color with some species routinely exhibiting more than one color form. Also mutations may occur that alter the hue or the color. Humans perceive color differently, especially subtle changes in hues. Film and the printing process can also affect color fidelity. It is therefore recommended that the reader check other color sections in the book when in doubt. Although highly complex and still not fully understood, flower color production remains a fascinating aspect of plant biology and a pleasing aesthetic that continues to nurture the human spirit. A brief and highly simplified overview of flower color follows. (Readers interested in a more detailed explanation of color in plants should refer to David Lee's book *Nature's Palette: The Science of Plant Color*.)

Structurally simple flowers generally display a single color. As the flower's structure increases in complexity, there is a greater likelihood that it will exhibit more than one color. In most cases, the petals are the most brightly colored part of the flower. Many flowers also exhibit contrasting colors, making them more noticeable to animals and potential pollinators. This is especially true for the sexual parts of a flower, namely the anthers and stigma. Varying shifts in color can be observed in some flowers after fertilization or during the aging process.

Winged Sumac in clear cut

Generally speaking, the most primitive flowers (those possessing the simplest structures) are yellow in color. Slightly more complex flowers tend to be white. Those that are structurally more advanced will often display red, pink, or purple flowers. The most advanced flowers are often blue in color or are composed of a mixture of colors. Colors become increasingly more complex as additional genes are involved in color production. For example, a yellow flower will have only the requisite genes needed to produce yellow while a blue flower requires the genetic determinants not only for yellow but also for white and red color production. This is why mutations in a blue flower can result in the production of a pink or even a white form. In some species, depending on the flower color of the parent, there is a natural tendency to revert to a less advanced color form. For example, white tends to revert to yellow, and pink or red may revert to white. Flowers are believed to have evolved from leaves and sometimes a reversion to the green color form of the ancestral leaf occurs. This event is solely the result of chance mutations and is independent of the normal starting color of the flower.

Flower color is produced either by pigments, surface structures, or a combination of the two. There are four metabolic pathways involved in the production of pigments in plants. The major classes of pigments involved in flower color production are the flavonoids and the carotenoids and, to a lesser extent, betalains and chlorophyll. The composition and concentration of these plant metabolites vary greatly among plant species, and most flower colors are produced from mixtures of pigments (referred to as "co-pigmentation"). Small changes in the relative proportion of pigments present can have a significant impact on the hue produced.

A second color-producing process referred to as "structural color" forms not through pigment production but by physical means. The surface structure of a petal as well as the distribution of intercellular spaces within the petal can strongly affect the color intensity of the flower. The formation of pure white color is a case in point. The flower petals of the Common Water Lily (*Nymphaea odorata*), a widespread and highly recognizable species, appear white but are actually colorless. The intense white coloration observed is produced by numerous tiny air spaces located within the tissue of the petals. These air spaces effectively scatter all wavelengths of light. When none of the wavelengths of light are absorbed, white light is reflected back. This accounts for the petal's coloration. If colored pigments are also present, then some light wavelengths may be absorbed. The air spaces in the petals could then act to diffuse the color's intensity. Pale colors can also result from the presence of fewer pigment molecules in each cell or fewer cells expressing the pigment.

A flower's coloration (along with shape, arrangement, and odor) can be correlated to its method of pollination. Very few flowers are green in color. They do not effectively stand out from the foliage and as such are usually not pollinated by animals. For example most grass flowers are usually not showy or brightly colored and are often inconspicuous. As such, the majority relies on wind as the primary mechanism of pollination. This method of pollination precludes requiring the plant to waste valuable metabolic energy on the production of large or brilliantly colored flowers. Things change, however, when animals have co-evolved to be the primary pollinators. The flower's color needs to lie within the spectrum of colors that a particular species or group of animals can detect. Pollinators are attracted to brightly colored flowers in hopes of finding a reward, namely nectar, a solution composed primarily of sugars that can sometimes be found in combination with a few lipids, amino acids, and the occasional vitamin.

Insects can detect ultraviolet light and see it as a separate color. Most insects (with the notable exception of some butterflies) cannot detect the red end of the visible light spectrum. Red appears to them as a kind of nondescript gray. Therefore, flowers pollinated

by insects tend to be yellow, orange, white, or blue. Many flowers have markings invisible to us. These markings reflect ultraviolet light and can be perceived by insects. This UV reflectance is believed to act as a guide, helping to direct an insect to the nectar source. Birds not only possess excellent color vision throughout the visible light range but, as recent studies have demonstrated, some can also see into the near UV and UV end of the spectrum. This allows birds to perceive many more colors than humans do. It is hypothesized that seeing UV light may aid birds in detection of potential prey, in foraging (as fruits and flowers may stand out more intensely against their background), and possibly in the evaluation of sexual selection cues. Those that are pollinators, such as hummingbirds, are very attracted to red, orange, and yellow flowers. They are also attracted to blue flowers but to a much lesser extent. This is due to colored oil droplets located in the color-sensing cells (cones) of the eyes that help to absorb some blue wavelengths of light, which aids in attenuating the glare coming from the sky.

Photographs

A photographic image accompanies each plant description, with a few species having a second image highlighting a flower color variant or a conspicuous and characteristic fruit. All of the photographs in the book were taken of plants in their natural habitat. Virginia Bluebell is the one exception. It was photographed at the Connecticut College Arboretum in New London, Connecticut. The photographs were made with Fuji or Kodak films using either a medium format or 35mm camera system.

Listings

The headings under each listing are as follows:

Common Name: The text for each species description begins with a common name. Common names are very popular, though they are also limited in their usefulness. Common names are usually regional and are often derived from some attribute of the plant such as color, habitat, or usefulness. Many species have multiple common names, and sometimes the same name may apply to several totally unrelated species. In short, the common name is not universal or specific in its recognition. Only one common name is presented for each species in this guide. Efforts have been made to select the most prevalent common name used in the region.

Cardinal Flowers growing in wet meadow

Fleabane and Queen Anne's Lace

Scientific Name: The scientific name, Latinized, is presented after the common name. Each species is given a single scientific name, unique to it and universally recognized. The scientific name is composed of two words. The first word is the genus and is indicative of a group of plants exhibiting similar characteristics. The second word is the specific epithet that identifies the individual species of plant. The genus name is always capitalized while the specific epithet is not. The genus name is generally a noun; and the specific epithet, an adjective that informs of the characteristic that separates this plant from other members of the same group.

Family Name: After the scientific name comes the common family name followed by the Latinized version. The Latinized family name is always capitalized and ends with the suffix "aceae." Members of a family share many similar traits and features. Recent advances in molecular biology have had a profound impact on plant classification. Many species sharing similar traits that botanists once thought were related have been shown to be distinct and separate while other seemingly unrelated species have been shown to possess an unexpected relationship to each other. What is acceptable nomenclature today may change tomorrow. All efforts have been made to reflect the current and proposed changes in plant families as found in the Angiosperm Phylogeny Web site as of 2007 (www.mobot.org/MOBOT/research/APweb/).

Description: This section briefly details the major physical characteristics of the plant that aid in delineating one species from another. These characteristics include the plant's size, stem, leaf and flower shape, and arrangement. Additional features such as roots, fruits, and other specialized structures are included in this section when such features are deemed useful in the identification process. Measurements are given, usually as a range, reflecting the variability inherent in biological systems. The measurements indicated are in feet, inches, and fractions of an inch. The descriptions have been kept to a minimum, as has the technical language. A glossary of terms is located near the end of the book.

Bloom Season: The bloom season for each plant is listed for a specific month or months. The reason for this approach is because of the significant range in the frost-free growing season in New England. Rainfall and snowfall in the region is fairly evenly distributed (with the exception of the mountain areas) at about 30 to 55 inches per year. The growing season is, however, affected by the length and severity of cold weather. The average frost-free growing season ranges from about 180 days in the southern part of the region to 120 days in the northernmost reaches of New England.

Habitat/Range: The habitat section provides information on the general types of environments favored by a particular species and provides an important link in the identification process. The range refers to the species geographic distribution within the region. Range is given by state, starting from the south to the north. The terms such as "common throughout the region" or "rare" refer to the relative abundance of the plant. While a number of sources were used to define the range of the species presented in this guide, the major source reference was the USDA Plants Database (http://plants.usda.gov/).

Comments: This section provides additional information about the species in question. The information may be about the plant's medicinal, commercial, or cultural uses or facts about the plant's region of origin or ecological role within a community. Any discussion of the medicinal uses for a given plant is reported here for historical purposes only. For those interested, the following Web sites provide additional information and related links: www.wildflower.org, native plants information from the Ladybird Johnson Wildflower Center; http://herb.umd.umich.edu, Native American Ethnobotany; www.newfs.org, New England Wildflower Society; http://nbii-nin.ciesin.columbia.edu/ipane/, Invasive Plant Atlas of New England.

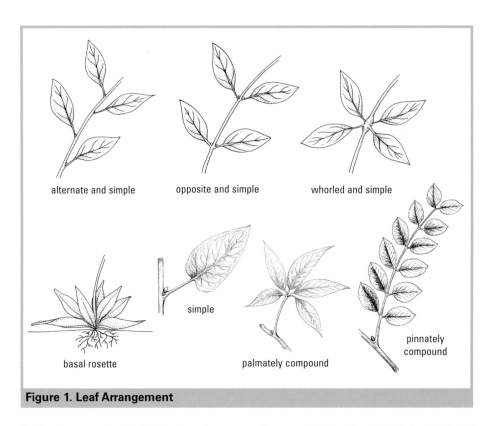

alternate and simple

opposite and simple

whorled and simple

basal rosette

simple

palmately compound

pinnately compound

Figure 1. Leaf Arrangement

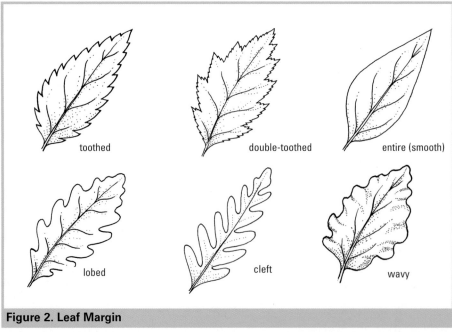

toothed

double-toothed

entire (smooth)

lobed

cleft

wavy

Figure 2. Leaf Margin

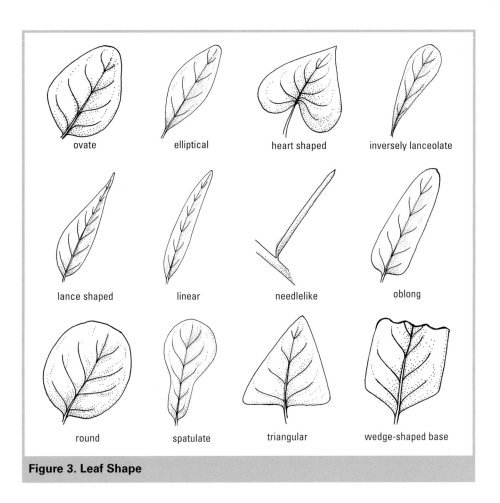

Figure 3. Leaf Shape

ovate · elliptical · heart shaped · inversely lanceolate

lance shaped · linear · needlelike · oblong

round · spatulate · triangular · wedge-shaped base

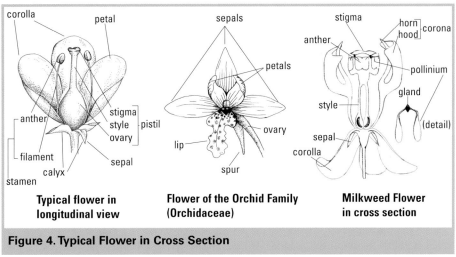

Typical flower in longitudinal view

corolla · petal · anther · stigma · style · ovary · pistil · filament · sepal · calyx · stamen

Flower of the Orchid Family (Orchidaceae)

sepals · petals · ovary · lip · spur

Milkweed Flower in cross section

stigma · horn · hood · corona · anther · pollinium · gland · style · (detail) · sepal · corolla

Figure 4. Typical Flower in Cross Section

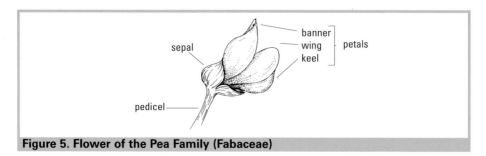

Figure 5. Flower of the Pea Family (Fabaceae)

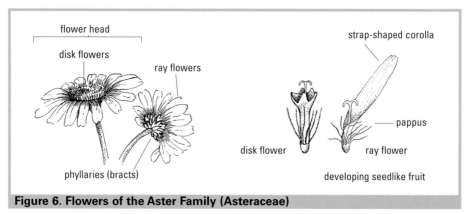

Figure 6. Flowers of the Aster Family (Asteraceae)

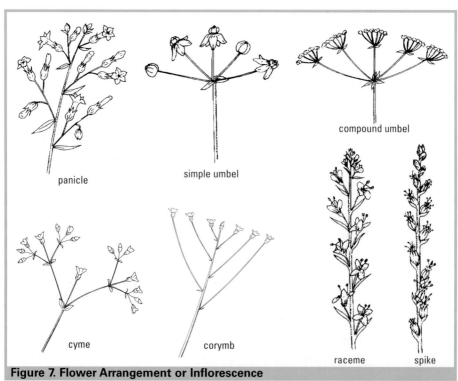

Figure 7. Flower Arrangement or Inflorescence

WHITE FLOWERS

This section includes flowers that range from bright white to a pale creamy white. White may also dominate in pale hues of yellow, pink, and blue, and those sections should also be checked.

ARROWHEAD
Sagittaria latifolia
Water Plantain Family (Alismataceae)

Description: An aquatic plant growing up to 30" long. The basal leaves are simple, arrow shaped, up to 12", stalked, with a smooth margin. The flowers appear on racemes and are white and ¾–1" wide, with a bright yellow center, 3 rounded petals, and 3 recurving green sepals.

Bloom Season: July–September.

Habitat/Range: *S. latifolia* can be found along streams and lakes, shallow pools, and various types of wet sites throughout the region.

Comments: Native Americans treated rheumatism with a leaf tea and indigestion with a tea made from the roots. The starchy tubers were eaten much like potatoes.

SOUTHERN WATER PLANTAIN
Alisma subcordatum
Water Plantain Family (Alismataceae)

Description: Plants are less than 3' tall and highly branched. The leaves are simple, basal, elliptic or ovate, up to 6" long, and stalked, with a smooth margin and distinct veins. The tiny white flowers are on terminal panicles. Each flower is ⅛–¼" with 3 white petals and 3 green sepals. Sepals and petals are of equal length.

Bloom Season: July–September.

Habitat/Range: The species grows in a variety of shallow water sites such as marshes and pond edges and along streams and can be found throughout the region.

Comments: Native Americans prepared a root tea to be used as a diuretic and a treatment for urinary and kidney ailments. A root poultice was also used in treating wounds.

WILD LEEK
Allium tricoccum
Onion Family (Alliaceae)

Description: Plants are 6–18" tall. The leaves emerge and die off well before the flowers emerge. The leaves are simple, basal (arising from a bulb), lanceolate to elliptic, and 6–12" long, with a smooth margin. Numerous flowers are found on terminal umbels, 1½–2" wide. The flowers are white, ⅛–¼", and cup shaped, with 3 petals and 3 sepals that are similar in hue.

Bloom Season: July–August.

Habitat/Range: Rich woodlands. Found throughout the region to central Maine.

Comments: The leaves and bulbs are both edible. The plant has a taste similar to garlic but significantly less potent.

BULBIFEROUS WATER HEMLOCK
Cicuta bulbifera
Umbel Family (Apiaceae)

Description: The plants are sparsely branched and reach a height of 1–3'. The leaves are alternate and pinnately compound, with each leaflet linear to narrowly ovate and variable in size, with the smaller leaves towards the top portion of the plant. The leaf margins are loosely toothed. Flowers are sparse or absent. When present, they are found in small compound umbels. Each umbel has 5–7 spokes. Individual flowers are approximately ⅛" wide, with 5 rounded petals. Small, round green bulblets can be found in the upper leaf axils.

Bloom Season: July–August.

Habitat/Range: Swamps and marshes throughout the region.

Comments: Bulblets can generate new plants, and their presence may help explain the low flower density. Caution: Like *C. maculata* the plant is highly poisonous.

WATER HEMLOCK
Cicuta maculata
Umbel Family (Apiaceae)

Description: This highly branched plant has a smooth green stem that is often streaked with purple marks or blotches and can grow to 6'' in height. The leaves are alternate and compound. The leaflets are narrowly ovate, 1–4" long, and sharply pointed at the tip, with a toothed margin. The veins of each leaflet end not at the tip of each tooth, but rather at the notches between the teeth. Numerous white flowers are borne on compound umbels. Individual flowers have 5 petals and measure ⅛" or less.

Bloom Season: July–August.

Habitat/Range: Swamps, marshes, and wet meadows. Found throughout the region.

Comments: All parts of this native species are highly poisonous. The poisonous component found in this plant is cicutoxin. When the plant is ingested, symptoms begin almost immediately. The toxin interferes with the central nervous system, and the victim usually dies within 20–30 minutes of respiratory failure. It has been reported that a single bite may be enough to kill an adult human. It is believed that those Native Americans wishing to commit suicide often did so by eating this plant.

QUEEN ANNE'S LACE
Daucus carota
Umbel Family (Apiaceae)

Description: A bristly plant, 10–36" in height, with a ribbed, hollow stem. The leaves are pinnately compound, 3–8" long and fernlike in appearance. The leaflets are linear to oblong with a toothed margin. The flowers are found on flat-topped compound umbels. Each umbel is 2–5" wide with 10–50 (or more) spokes. The creamy white flowers are less than ¼" wide with 5 petals and 5 smaller green sepals. At the center of each umbel, there is a reddish purple flower. The exact function of the purple flower is still a mystery. After fertilization and during seed development, the bracts begin curving upward. This motion closes the flower head and results in its characteristic nestlike appearance.

Bloom Season: July–September.

Habitat/Range: Fields, meadows, roadsides, and weeds. Commonly found throughout the region.

Comments: This European introduction is believed by many botanists to be the ancestor to the modern-day, garden-variety carrot. Traditional folk medicine used a root tea as a diuretic, to treat urinary stones, and expel worms. The seeds were also used as a "morning after" contraceptive. Handling the plant can cause dermatitis in sensitive individuals. A wine was made from it in Britain, and Germans used it as a coffee substitute.

COW PARSNIP

Heracleum maximum
Umbel Family (Apiaceae)

Description: A large, hollow-stemmed, woolly plant that can grow up to 10' tall. The leaves are alternate and trifoliate, with each leaflet superficially resembling a maple leaf. They reach a length of 4–12" and are lobed and coarsely toothed. Numerous white flowers are found on large umbels that are 4–10" wide and made up of 15–30 spokes. Each flower is ¼–½" with 5 notched petals.

Bloom Season: June–July.

Habitat/Range: Rich, moist soils. Found throughout the region.

Comments: Native Americans used a root tea preparation to combat coughs, colds, colic, cramps, headaches, and sore throats. This species could be confused with Water Hemlock (*Circuta maculata*), a species that is highly poisonous.

SPREADING DOGBANE

Apocynum androsaemifolium
Dogbane Family (Apocynaceae)

Description: A somewhat bushy plant containing a milky sap and growing 6–30". The blue-green leaves are simple, opposite, elliptic or ovate, 1–3" long, stalked, drooping, and with a smooth margin. The flowers are found on terminal panicles. They are white to pale pink, nodding, ¼–⅜". Each flower is bell shaped with spreading or recurving lobes and is striped with a darker pink on the inside.

Bloom Season: July–August.

Habitat/Range: Fields, thickets, and roadsides throughout the region.

Comments: These poisonous plants are related to the milkweeds (Asclepias Family). Ingestion of the plant by humans and other mammals will cause vomiting. The milky sap contains the toxic cardiac glycoside cymarin. Although primarily milkweed feeders, Monarch Butterfly larvae will feed on Dogbane. Native Americans used the roots for a variety of medicinal purposes.

INDIAN HEMP

Apocynum cannabinum
Dogbane Family (Apocynaceae)

Description: Loosely branching plants 2–5' tall containing a milky sap. The leaves are simple, opposite, lance shaped, 2–4" long, and sessile or short stalked, with a smooth margin. The flowers are found in small clusters. The greenish white flowers are bell shaped, ⅛–¼", with 5 erect (or slightly spreading) lobes.

Bloom Season: July–August.

Habitat/Range: Woodland edges, thickets, and stream banks. Found throughout the region.

Comments: Native Americans used the berries and roots to treat heart ailments. The plants contain active cardiac glycosides. Plants are poisonous to livestock. The milky sap was used in folk medicine as a means of treating venereal warts. The fibrous stem was used to make cordage.

TALL MILKWEED
Asclepias exalta
Dogbane Family (Apocynaceae)

Description: Erect plants 2–6' in height. The leaves are simple, opposite, elliptic or ovate, and 2–10" long, with a smooth margin and a hairy underside. A few flowers are on umbels. Individual flowers are white, nodding, and ⅜–½", with 5 united petals that have reflexed lobes and a crownlike center.

Bloom Season: June–early August.

Habitat/Range: Found in moist rich uplands throughout the region.

Comments: *A. exalta* is one of the earliest milkweeds to bloom in the region. All parts of the plant are poisonous due to the presence of cardiac glycosides.

WILD SARSAPARILLA
Aralia nudicaulis
Ginseng Family (Araliaceae)

Description: Plants are erect, 5–15", and hairless. The solitary leaf is basal and divided into 3 groups, with 3–5 leaflets per group. Each leaflet is ovate and up to 6" long, with a pointed tip and toothed margin. The leaflets rise above the flower stalk. Flowers are greenish white and generally on 3 umbels arising from a single stalk. Each circular cluster of flowers measures 1–2" in diameter. The flower stalk is leafless. Individual flowers are inconspicuous and about ⅛" wide, with 5 reflexed petals.

Bloom Season: May.

Habitat/Range: Woodlands. Found throughout the region.

Comments: Native Americans made a drink from the roots. A root tea was used to treat ailments ranging from general malaise to coughs and stomachaches.

DWARF GINSENG
Panax trifolius
Ginseng Family (Araliaceae)

Description: A small plant, 3–8" tall. Leaves are in whorls of 3 and divided into 3 (or occasionally 5) leaflets. Each leaflet is oblong to narrowly ovate, 1–2" long, sessile with a toothed margin. The white to pinkish yellow flowers are on small, round terminal umbels. The tiny flowers measure ¹⁄₁₆" and have 5 petals and 5 sepals.

Bloom Season: May.

Habitat/Range: Rich, moist woodlands. Commonly found throughout the region to southern Maine.

Comments: Native Americans made a whole plant tea to combat colic, indigestion, rheumatism, and tuberculosis. The raw root was chewed as a remedy for headaches. The tuber can be eaten either cooked or raw.

YARROW
Achillea millefolium
Composite Family (Asteraceae)

Description: Plants range in size from 6–36" and the stem is usually covered with fine hairs. The lanceolate leaves are finely dissected, giving the plant a fernlike appearance. They are sessile, gray-green in color, and 1–6" long. When crushed, the leaves release a highly fragrant odor. Basal leaves are longer than the upper leaves. Numerous flower heads are found on flat panicles. The flowers are white and have 5 petal-like rays that surround the central disk. Individual flowers are up to ⅜" wide.

Bloom Season: June–September.

Habitat/Range: Pastures, fields, and roadsides. Commonly found throughout the region.

Comments: The Latin name of this plant is derived from ancient Greek legend. It was named after the warrior Achilles who, it was said, used the plant to heal soldiers' wounds during the Trojan War. Native Americans prepared a leaf tea to treat stomach disorders and reduce fevers and colds. Crushed leaves were applied to fresh cuts to stop the bleeding. The active ingredient is achilleine. Handling the plant has been reported to cause a skin irritation in sensitive individuals. Whether this plant species is native to North America or a European introduction is still in dispute.

WHITE SNAKEROOT
Ageratina altissima
Composite Family (Asteraceae)

Description: *A. altissima* is an erect plant, 1–4' tall. The leaves are simple, opposite, heart shaped to ovate, 2–6" long, and slender stalked, with a pointed tip and toothed margin. The flower heads are on dense panicles and average 10–20 flowers per cluster. Individual flower heads are white, measure ⅛–¼" wide, lack ray flowers, and have a fuzzy appearance.

Bloom Season: July–September.

Habitat/Range: Woodlands and thickets. Found throughout the region.

Comments: The plant is poisonous.

PEARLY EVERLASTING
Anaphalis margaritacea
Composite Family (Asteraceae)

Description: An erect plant, 6–30" tall, with a white woolly stem and gray-green down-covered foliage. The simple leaves are alternate, narrowly ovate to linear, 2–4" long, and sessile, with a smooth margin that is often rolled under. The leaves are gray-green on the upper surface and white-woolly below. Numerous flowers are found on short, flat-topped panicles. Each rayless flower head is ovate and ¼" wide, with a yellow center that is surrounded by white petal-like bracts.

Bloom Season: July–August.

Habitat/Range: Fields, roadsides, and dry open areas. Found throughout the region.

Comments: Native Americans prepared a whole-plant tea to treat a variety of upper respiratory ailments. Today, the plant is frequently used in dried-flower arrangements.

FIELD PUSSYTOES
Antennaria neglecta
Composite Family (Asteraceae)

Description: Field Pussytoes is a plant 3–12" tall that often forms mats. The leaves are simple, basal, and narrowly ovate to spoon shaped with smooth margins. The 1–2" long leaves have a single prominent vein and are densely hairy on the underside and sparsely hairy on the topside. There are usually 3–10 stem leaves with roughly the same general appearance as the basal leaves except that they are smaller. Several white flowers are found on terminal heads. Individual flowers are ¼". Male and female flowers reside on separate plants.

Bloom Season: May–June.

Habitat/Range: Fields and woodlands, especially rocky outcroppings and open slopes. Found throughout the region.

Comments: This species is highly variable. It was used in folk medicine to treat colds and snakebites.

PLANTAIN-LEAVED PUSSYTOES
Antennaria plantaginifolia
Composite Family (Asteraceae)

Description: This native species grows up to 15"
tall and is woolly stemmed. The basal leaves are
spoon shaped and 1½–3" long, with a smooth
margin. Each leaf has 3–5 prominent veins and is
densely white-hairy on the upper surface and less
so underneath. Several flower heads are found in
terminal clusters. The heads are up to ¾" wide
and rayless and have a fuzzy appearance. The
bracts are green and tipped in white. Male and
female flowers are found on separate plants.

Bloom Season: May–June.

Habitat/Range: Open woodlands, meadows, and
dry areas. Found throughout the region.

Comments: This native plant spreads by runners,
often forming dense colonies in the process.
This plant was used in folk medicine to treat
ailments such as diarrhea, lung problems, and
even snakebites.

TALL FLAT-TOPPED WHITE ASTER
Doellingeria umbellata
Composite Family (Asteraceae)

Description: A hairless or nearly hairless aster
that can grow up to 7' in height. The leaves are
simple, alternate, elliptic to ovate, 2–6" long, and
sessile, with a smooth margin. Numerous flower
heads are found on flat-topped panicles. Each
head is ¼–⅝" wide with 7–15 white rays and a
yellow central disk.

Bloom Season: August–October.

Habitat/Range: Moist woodlands, wet meadows,
and thickets throughout the region.

Comments: Native Americans used leaf infusions
to treat stomach disorders.

PILEWORT

Erechtites hieraciifolia
Composite Family (Asteraceae)

Description: These strong-smelling plants can reach up to 8' in height. The leaves are simple, alternate, elliptic or ovate, 2–8" long, and short stalked and with a pointed tip and toothed margin. The upper stem leaves are clasping. The flower heads are numerous and are found on panicles. Each head is ½–¾" and cylinder shaped, with a swollen base. Numerous tiny 5-lobed white flowers are contained in each head.

Bloom Season: July–August.

Habitat/Range: Found in a variety of habitats but has a special fondness for disturbed sites. Common throughout the region.

Comments: Native Americans used the whole plant for a variety of medicinal purposes.

DAISY FLEABANE

Erigeron strigosus
Composite Family (Asteraceae)

Description: Erect plants, 1–2½' tall and hairy stemmed. The basal leaves are simple, elliptic or ovate, up to 5" long, and stalked, with a smooth or toothed margin. Stem leaves are alternate, narrowly ovate to linear in shape, hairless, and sessile. The flower heads are found in branched clusters, several to many, each up to ½–1" wide. The central disk is yellow and is surrounded by 50–100 white rays that are short in length with respect to the width of the disk. Involucral bracts are hairy.

Bloom Season: May–September.

Habitat/Range: Fields, thickets, weedy and disturbed areas. Common throughout the region.

Comments: Folklore has it that the flower heads, when dried and placed throughout the interior of a home, could rid the dwelling of fleas.

BONESET
Eupatorium perfoliatum
Composite Family (Asteraceae)

Description: Plants are erect, 2–4' tall, and hairy. The leaves are opposite, simple, narrowly ovate, and 2–8" long, with a pointed tip and a toothed margin. In addition, the leaves completely encircle the stem (known as perfoliate leaves). The flower heads are on dense, flat-topped panicles. Individual heads are about ¼" wide, white in color, devoid of rays, and filamentous in appearance.

Bloom Season: July–August.

Habitat/Range: Found in thickets, fields, swamps, and moist, low, wet ground throughout the region.

Comments: Native Americans, as well as early settlers, used the leaves to treat ailments such as rheumatism, malaria, muscle pains, and colds. A cautionary note: This plant is believed to contain a number of potentially harmful alkaloids that could, if ingested, adversely affect liver function.

WHITE WOOD ASTER
Eurybia divaricata
Composite Family (Asteraceae)

Description: Plants with a stem that frequently has a zigzag shape to it and grows 1–3' tall. The leaves are simple, alternate, heart shaped, 1–6" long, and stalked, with a pointed tip, notched base, and coarsely toothed margin. The flower heads are located on flat-topped panicles. Individual heads are ¾–1" wide with 5–16 white rays and a central disk that ranges from yellow to purple. The disk flowers are tube shaped with 5 lobes.

Bloom Season: August–October.

Habitat/Range: Dry woodlands. Found throughout Connecticut, Rhode Island, Massachusetts, Vermont, and New Hampshire.

Comments: The seeds of this shade-tolerant woodland species provide a valuable food resource for several species of birds, including goldfinches and sparrows.

COMMON QUICKWEED
Galinsoga quadriradiata
Composite Family (Asteraceae)

Description: This highly branching plant grows 6–24" tall and has a hairy stem. The leaves are simple, ovate, and 1–3" long, with a finely toothed margin. Numerous flower heads, white with a yellow center, are borne on open panicles. Individual flowers measure ¼". The 4–5 petal-like rays are toothed.

Bloom Season: Late June–October.

Habitat/Range: Weedy places, fields, and waste areas. Found throughout the region.

Comments: This species is a European introduction and has become extremely common in the northeastern United States.

OX-EYE DAISY
Leucanthemum vulgare
Composite Family (Asteraceae)

Description: This European introduction grows 6–30" tall and is hairless. The dark green basal leaves are simple, alternate, spoon shaped or ovate, 1–6" long, and stalked, with a toothed or lobed margin. The stem leaves are oblong to ovate and measure up to 3" long. The solitary flower heads measure 1–2" wide and are composed of 15–30 white rays and a yellow central disk containing numerous disk flowers.

Bloom Season: Late May–July.

Habitat/Range: Fields, meadows, weedy areas, and roadsides. Found throughout the region.

Comments: Europeans used extracts of the plant to induce vomiting, to help in regulating menses, and to act as a diuretic. Native Americans treated fevers with a tea prepared from the flowers.

CLIMBING HEMPWEED
Mikania scandens
Composite Family (Asteraceae)

Description: A climbing vine that can reach a length of 15'. The leaves are simple, opposite, somewhat triangular in shape, and 1–5" long, with a notched base and slightly toothed margin. The flower heads are in branching, flat-topped clusters arising from leaf axils. The white to pink heads are ¼" wide and composed of 4 disk flowers.

Bloom Season: July–August.

Habitat/Range: Swamps, wet thickets, and stream banks. Found in Connecticut, Rhode Island, and Massachusetts to southern Vermont, New Hampshire, and Maine.

Comments: Frequently referred to as Climbing Boneset due to the similarity of its flowers to those of Boneset (*E. perfoliatum*).

WHORLED ASTER
Oclemena acuminata
Composite Family (Asteraceae)

Description: The plants range in size from 6–30" and are hairy. The leaves are found in irregular whorls with each leaf elliptic or ovate and 2–6" in length, with a long pointed tip and a smooth margin. The flower heads, several to many, are found on flat-topped panicles. The heads range in color from white to pale pink and average ¾–1" with 10–20 rays.

Bloom Season: July–August.

Habitat/Range: Woodlands throughout the region.

Comments: This is the first aster species to bloom in the region.

TALL WHITE LETTUCE
Prenanthes altissima
Composite Family (Asteraceae)

Description: Plants are 1–6' tall and usually hairless. The highly variable leaves range from ovate to triangular, and are 1–6" long and often deeply lobed. The leaf base is usually notched and the margin is frequently toothed. As leaves ascend the stem, they are reduced in size. The whitish-colored flower heads are found in axillary and terminal clusters. The heads are nodding and up to ¾" long.

Bloom Season: July–August.

Habitat/Range: Moist woodlands. Found throughout the region.

Comments: Native Americans used a root poultice to treat rattlesnake bites.

TOOTHED WHITE-TOPPED ASTER
Sericocarpus asteroides
Composite Family (Asteraceae)

Description: Plants range from 6–24" and are hairy. The leaves can appear spoon shaped or narrowly ovate, broader at the tip, ½–4" long, sometimes hairy or fringed, and stalked, with a smooth margin. The upper leaves are sessile. The flower heads form on flat-topped panicles. Each head is ½" wide with 4–8 white rays surrounding a central disk.

Bloom Season: July–August.

Habitat/Range: Dry woodlands. Found in Connecticut, Rhode Island, and Massachusetts to central Vermont and New Hampshire.

Comments: This species is extremely rare in Maine, being at the northern limits of its range.

SILVERROD
Solidago bicolor
Composite Family (Asteraceae)

Description: Hairy plants, 4–36" in height. The leaves are simple, alternate, ovate or elliptic, and hairy, with a toothed margin. The flower heads are on elongated panicles 3–9" tall. Each head is ¼" wide with 7–10 white rays. Involucral bracts are white with a green band.

Bloom Season: July–October.

Habitat/Range: Found in dry woodlands and open, rocky areas throughout the region.

Comments: This is the only goldenrod species in New England with white rays. Hairy Goldenrod (*S. hispida*) looks nearly identical to Silverrod except for its yellow rays.

HEATH ASTER
Symphyotrichum ericoides
Composite Family (Asteraceae)

Description: Plants are highly branched, 1–3', and hairy. The linear leaves are less than 2" long and have a smooth margin. The flower heads are found on one-sided branches. Distribution of the heads along the branches ranges from sparse to tightly packed. The flowers are ¼–½" wide with a yellow to reddish central disk and 8–20 white or pale pink rays. The bracts have blunted tips and spread away from their base.

Bloom Season: July–September.

Habitat/Range: Grows in dry open areas such as fields. Commonly found in Connecticut, Rhode Island, and Massachusetts and in a few scattered locations in Vermont, New Hampshire, and Maine.

Comments: Heath Aster has the ability to grow in a wide variety of soil types.

PANICLED ASTER
Symphyotrichum lanceolatum
Composite Family (Asteraceae)

Description: A tall-stemmed aster ranging from 2–7'. The leaves are simple, alternate, linear to narrowly ovate, 2–6" long, and pointed at the tip. They may be stalked or sessile and usually have a toothed margin. Numerous flower heads are found on panicles. Each flower head is ¾–1" wide with 20–40 rays. The rays can range in color from white to pale purple to light blue. Flower heads are individually stalked. Involucral bracts are green and pointed.

Bloom Season: August–October.

Habitat/Range: Thickets, meadows, shorelines, and other moist areas. Found throughout the region.

Comments: Panicled Aster spreads by means of rhizomes and can form large colonies.

CALICO ASTER
Symphyotrichum lateriflorum
Composite Family (Asteraceae)

Description: This plant is somewhat scraggly looking, 1–5' tall, and hairy or hairless. The leaves are simple, linear, or narrowly ovate, up to 5" long, and slightly tapered at both ends, with a smooth or slightly toothed margin. The lower leaves are stalked and the upper ones are sessile. The flower heads occur on broad panicles and are usually found along one side of the branch. The central disk is yellow or purple and is surrounded by 9–15 white or pale purple rays. Each head is ¼–½" wide.

Bloom Season: July–September.

Habitat/Range: Found in fields, meadows, and open woodlands throughout the region.

Comments: This native species' common name comes from the fact that many plants sport both yellow and purple flower heads at the same time.

AWL ASTER

Symphyotrichum pilosum
Composite Family (Asteraceae)

Description: A spindly, clump-forming plant, up to 4' tall, with numerous branches. The lower part of the stems can become semi-woody with age. The leaves are simple, alternate, linear, ½–3" long, and, sessile, with sharp, pointed tips and a smooth margin. The flower heads are on 1-sided branches. Each head is short stalked, ¼–¾" wide, with 15–30 white rays surrounding the central disk. The involucral bracts have a somewhat triangular shape and are hairless.

Bloom Season: July–October.

Habitat/Range: Dry fields, waste areas, and various open areas. Found in Connecticut, Rhode Island, and Massachusetts to southern Vermont, New Hampshire, and Maine.

Comments: *S. pilosum* can be an aggressive colonizer, especially in abandoned fields where it can dominate for several years.

SMALL WHITE-FLOWERED ASTER

Symphyotrichum racemosum
Composite Family (Asteraceae)

Description: Highly branching plants, 1–5' tall, hairless or hairy, and often with a purple-tinged stem. The leaves are linear or narrowly ovate, up to 4" long, pointed at the tip, and sessile, with a smooth margin. Stem leaves are consistently larger than those found on the branches. Numerous flower heads abound on open panicles and are clustered to one side of the branch. Each head is ¼–⅜" wide with 15–30 white rays surrounding a yellow or pinkish central disk.

Bloom Season: August–October.

Habitat/Range: Woodlands, fields, meadows, and shorelines. Found throughout the region to central Maine.

Comments: Asters are typically pollinated by a variety of insect species from butterflies and moths to bees and flies.

MAYAPPLE

Podophyllum peltatum
Barberry Family (Berberidaceae)

Description: Mayapple is often found growing in dense patches. Plants are 12–18" tall with 2 leaves. The leaves are somewhat round in shape and deeply notched into lobes, averaging 3–7 per leaf. The large leaves are 10–12" wide with a toothed margin and short stalked. The leaves are attached at about midstem. A solitary flower rises from the fork between the leaves. The flower is white, nodding, and 1–2" wide with 6 or 9 waxy petals.

Bloom Season: Late April–early June.

Habitat/Range: Rich woodlands and thickets. Found in Vermont, New Hampshire, western Massachusetts, and western Connecticut.

Comments: Native Americans and the early colonists used extracts made from the roots to treat constipation, fevers, and syphilis. In addition, the root extracts were also used as a worm expellant. The most toxic part of the plant, the rhizome, contains high levels of podophyllotoxin and alpha and beta peltatin. These compounds have been shown to exhibit anticancer activity. Two major modern-day drugs were derived from podophyllo-toxin—etoposide and teniposide. Both compounds have been used to treat specific types of cancer. Simply handling either the rhizome or the stem may cause dermatitis in sensitive individuals.

SHEPHERD'S PURSE

Capsella bursa-pastoris
Mustard Family (Brassicaceae)

Description: An erect plant, 6–24" tall, unbranched or with several branches. There is a rosette of basal leaves. Each leaf is 2–4" long, oblong and lobed, smooth textured or hairy, appearing almost dandelion-like. The stem leaves are alternate, arrow shaped, clasping, and smaller than the basal leaves, and may or may not have a toothed margin. The flowers are on racemes. The flower, up to ⅛", has 4 white petals and 4 greenish sepals.

Bloom Season: May–October.

Habitat/Range: Roadsides, waste areas, and disturbed sites. Commonly found throughout the region.

Comments: This European introduction is a serious weed of cultivated areas. European folk medicine used teas made from the seeds and leaves to stop bleeding and as a diuretic. It was also used during childbirth. Modern research has shown that plant extracts contain uterine-contracting agents.

CUT-LEAF TOOTHWORT
Cardamine concatenata
Mustard Family (Brassicaceae)

Description: Plants generally range from 8–18"
tall. Leaves are narrow, 2–5" long, deeply lobed,
sharp-toothed, and arranged in whorls of 3
situated roughly above midstem. The flowers are
on terminal clusters 1–1½" wide. Individual
flowers are white (or sometimes pale pink) with 4
petals, ½–¾" long.

Bloom Season: Late April–May.

Habitat/Range: Rich moist woodlands and
thickets. Found throughout region except in
Maine.

Comments: The toothlike projections found on the
underground stems were not only the source for
its common name but also for its use as a folk
remedy for toothaches. In addition, a root tea was
used to treat sore throats. The peppery-tasting
rhizome can be chopped for use in a salad.

COMMON BITTERCRESS
Cardamine pensylvanica
Mustard Family (Brassicaceae)

Description: A slightly hairy plant, 4–24" in
height. The few basal leaves are somewhat ovate
and divided into narrow lobes. There are 2–12
leaflets, ½–¾" wide. The 4–10 stem leaves are
1–3" long and divided into 2–10 narrow leaflets.
The flowers are found on racemes. Each small
white flower measures about ⅟₁₆" wide and is
stalked. There are 4 petals and 4 sepals present.

Bloom Season: Late April–June.

Habitat/Range: Found in wet woodlands,
swamps, and meadows, and along shorelines.
Common throughout the region.

Comments: The leaves of this native species are
edible and have often been used in salads.

WILD PEPPERGRASS
Lepidium virginicum
Mustard Family (Brassicaceae)

Description: The plants are branched and erect, reaching up to 30" in height. The basal leaves are narrowly ovate, deeply lobed, and up to 2" long. Stem leaves are smaller, linear, and stalked, with a smooth margin. Numerous tiny flowers are located on dense racemes. The inconspicuous white flower measures less than ⅛" and has 4 petals and 2 stamens.

Bloom Season: May–October.

Habitat/Range: Fields, roadsides, and weedy areas. Common throughout the region.

Comments: Native Americans used a leaf tea to treat scurvy and to reduce the severity of poison-ivy rash.

TARTARIAN HONEYSUCKLE
Lonicera tartarica
Honeysuckle Family (Caprifoliaceae)

Description: A 4–10' tall, erect, branching shrub. The leaves are simple, opposite, somewhat ovate, 1–2½" long, and with a smooth margin. The flowers range in color from white to pink to yellow and average 3¾" in length. The long-stalked flowers are found as axial pairs. The corolla is tubular, hairy inside, and 2 lipped, with 5 petal-like lobes of unequal length.

Bloom Season: May–June.

Habitat/Range: Found along the edges of fields and thickets throughout the region.

Comments: Introduced from Eurasia, it has escaped cultivation and has become well established in the eastern United States.

ELDERBERRY

Sambucus canadensis
Honeysuckle Family (Caprifoliaceae)

Description: A medium-sized branching shrub, 9–12' tall. The leaves are opposite, pinnately compound, with 5–11 leaflets. Each leaflet is elliptic to lanceolate and 2–6" long, and with a toothed margin. Numerous tiny white flowers are found on flat-topped clusters 2–10" wide. Individual flowers are 5-lobed and measure approximately ⅛".

Bloom Season: June–July.

Habitat/Range: Found along the edges of fields and thickets as well as low wet places throughout the region.

Comments: Native Americans used a bark tea as a diuretic and emetic and used leaves on bruises and bleeding cuts. The berries are an important food source for many bird species and can also be made into a rather tasty jelly.

ARROWWOOD

Viburnum dentatum
Honeysuckle Family (Caprifoliaceae)

Description: This erect shrub, 3–15' tall, is branched with downy twigs. The leaves are simple, opposite, narrowly ovate to ovate, and 1–3" long, and with a rounded or heart-shaped base and a coarsely toothed margin. The small white flowers are found in a flat-topped cluster, 3–5" in diameter. Each flower is ¼" wide with 5 petals.

Bloom Season: May–August.

Habitat/Range: Woodland borders and thickets. Found throughout the region.

Comments: This shrub's common name was derived from the fact that the plant's long, straight branches were used as a source for making arrows.

HOBBLEBUSH
Viburnum lantanoides
Honeysuckle Family (Caprifoliaceae)

Description: A medium-sized shrub, 3–10' tall. The leaves are simple, opposite, heart shaped, 2–8" long, with a series of prominent veins, a finely toothed margin, and conspicuous brownish-colored hairs on the underside. Numerous white flowers are found on flat-topped clusters. Each cluster is 2–5" wide. Two types of flowers are present. On the outer periphery of the cluster are large, showy flowers, about 1" wide, with 5 petals. These flowers are sterile. The small central flowers have 5 petal-like lobes and are fertile.

Bloom Season: April–May.

Habitat/Range: Found in woodlands throughout the region.

Comments: This native shrub often forms dense stands and serves as both an important food source and cover for wildlife.

MOUSE-EAR CHICKWEED

Cerastium fontanum

Pink Family (Caryophyllaceae)

Description: The plants are prostrate and spreading, about 6–24" and prominently hairy. The leaves are simple, opposite, oblong to ovate, ½–1" long, sessile, and hairy. The flowers are on panicles. Each flower is white and ¼" wide, with 5 petals that are deeply notched and 5 green sepals. The petals are smaller than or equal to the length of the sepals.

Bloom Season: May–October.

Habitat/Range: Fields, roadsides, and waste areas. Found throughout the region.

Comments: A common species in the region originally introduced from Europe. The stems can root at the nodes, allowing it to form dense mats.

BOUNCING BET

Saponaria officinalis

Pink Family (Caryophyllaceae)

Description: These plants grow up to 3' tall and have a smooth stem. The leaves are simple, opposite, narrowly ovate, and 2–4" long, with a pointed tip, smooth margin, and 3–5 prominent veins. Many fragrant flowers are found on dense panicles. The flower color ranges from white to pink to pale blue. Each flower is ½–1" wide with 5 notched petals that are often reflexed and 5 sepals.

Bloom Season: Late June–September.

Habitat/Range: Fields, roadsides, and weedy or disturbed areas. Found throughout the region.

Comments: Originally introduced into North America from Europe. It has a spreading underground stem and can form large, dense colonies, often outcompeting many native species. The plant contains a number of saponins. These are soaplike compounds that are poisonous. Moths are the primary pollinators.

WHITE CAMPION
Silene latifolia
Pink Family (Caryophyllaceae)

Description: An erect, branching plant, 8–24".
The leaves are simple, opposite, and narrowly
ovate or ovate with a smooth margin. The leaves
are hairy, range in size from 1–3" long, and are
often clasping the stem. The flowers are scented
and white to pale pinkish white, and found on
open panicles. Each flower measures ½–1". The 5
petals are highly lobed and the 5 green sepals are
fused and inflated and display prominent
venation. This gives them a balloonlike
appearance. Male and female flowers are on
separate plants.

Bloom Season: May–July.

Habitat/Range: Fields and weedy areas.
Commonly found throughout the region.

Comments: This European introduction is
primarily a night-blooming species, with moths
acting as the main pollinators.

BLADDER CAMPION
Silene vulgaris
Pink Family (Caryophyllaceae)

Description: Plants grow to 30". The leaves
and stem are hairless. Leaves are opposite,
ovate to elliptic, 1–4" long, and often clasping
the stem. Flowers, few to many, are found on
open panicles. The flower has 5 white petals
that are deeply notched into 2 lobes each and
5 fused sepals that are highly inflated with
prominent veins.

Bloom Season: May–September.

Habitat/Range: Fields, waste areas, and
roadsides. Commonly found throughout the
region.

Comments: Originally from Europe, this species
has naturalized throughout the region. The stem,
unlike White Campion, is not branched. The
flowers open at night and are pollinated primarily
by moths.

STAR CHICKWEED
Stellaria pubera
Pink Family (Caryophyllaceae)

Description: Plants grow 6–18", erect or ascending. The leaves are simple, opposite, narrowly ovate, 1–4" long, and sessile, with a smooth margin. The flowers are found on panicles arising from leaf axils. The white flowers are ½" wide with 5 petals that are so deeply notched that there appear to be 10 petals. The 5 green sepals are shorter than the petals.

Bloom Season: April–May.

Habitat/Range: Rich woodlands and rocky slopes. Found scattered throughout Connecticut, Massachusetts, and Vermont.

Comments: This forest species is considered by many to be the showiest of the many chickweed species growing in the region.

SWEET PEPPERBUSH
Clethra alnifolia
Clethra Family (Clethraceae)

Description: A medium-sized branching shrub, 3–10' tall. The leaves are simple, alternate, 1–3" long, with a toothed margin above the middle of the leaf and a smooth margin below the middle. Numerous fragrant white flowers reside on upright terminal clusters. Each flower is ⅜" wide, with 5 rounded petals and a protruding style.

Bloom Season: July–August.

Habitat/Range: Moist woodlands, swamps, and other wetlands. Found throughout the region.

Comments: The flowers of Sweet Pepperbush provide an important nectar source for a variety of insects during the summer.

HEDGE BINDWEED

Calystegia sepium

Morning-Glory Family (Convolvulaceae)

Description: This native vine reaches lengths of 3–10' with large, morning-glorylike flowers. The leaves are simple, alternate, and distinctively triangular, with blunt lobes and smooth margins. Leaves range in size from 2–4". The solitary (or several) flowers rise from leaf axils and are long stalked (2–5"). They range in color from pink with 5 white stripes to all white. Individual flowers are 1½–3" long. Each flower has 2 stigmas and is funnel shaped due to its 5 united petals.

Bloom Season: May–July.

Habitat/Range: Moist soils, fields, thickets, and roadsides. Quite common throughout the region.

Comments: Native Americans used the root of Hedge Bindweed as a purgative and also for the treatment of gallbladder ailments.

COMMON DODDER

Cuscuta gronovii

Morning-Glory Family (Convolvulaceae)

Description: The chlorophyll-lacking Common Dodder is a parasitic vine with a threadlike, bright yellow to orange stem that is found readily twining around other plants. The leaves are either completely absent or reduced to tiny scales. The white flowers are found in dense clusters scattered along the stem. Individual flowers are ¼" wide with 5 petals and 5 sepals.

Bloom Season: August–early October.

Habitat/Range: Parasitic on a wide variety of plants and found throughout the region.

Comments: This native species can cause severe damage to a wide range of plants, including agricultural crops. The bright colors (yellow, orange, or red) of the stems are due to the presence of high levels of carotenoids.

BUNCHBERRY
Cornus canadensis
Dogwood Family (Cornaceae)

Description: This diminutive member of the Dogwood Family reaches a maximum height of about 8". The dark green leaves are simple and arranged in whorls of 4 or 6. Each short-stalked leaf is ovate, with a pointed tip, prominent parallel veins, and smooth margin, and measures 1–3" in length. Only flowering plants have whorls of 6 leaves. Those with whorls of 4 leaves are sterile. A stalked, round cluster of numerous tiny yellow-green flowers rises above the leaf whorl. The flower cluster is surrounded by a set of 4 large white bracts, giving the plant the appearance of having large flowers.

Bloom Season: June–July.

Habitat/Range: Moist woodlands and bogs. Common throughout the region.

Comments: This shade-tolerant shrub was named for the clusters of red berries it produces. Native Americans made a tea from the leaves and used it to treat aches and pains as well as coughs and kidney ailments, and a root tea to treat infant colic. The edible berries were often stored and used as a food resource during the winter months.

SPATULATE-LEAVED SUNDEW
Drosera intermedia
Sundew Family (Droseraceae)

Description: These are tiny and somewhat fragile-looking plants that range from 2–8". The leaves are simple, basal, spoon shaped, broadest at the tip, erect, 2–8" in length, and long stalked, with a smooth margin. Each leaf is covered with numerous reddish, sticky, glandular hairs. One to as many as 20 white (sometimes pink) flowers can be found on a 1-sided coiled raceme. Individual flowers are ¼" wide and have 5 petals. Usually only 1 or 2 flowers are open at any one time.

Bloom Season: July–August.

Habitat/Range: Wet areas generally with nutrient-poor, acidic soils such as bogs and wet sandy areas. Found throughout the region.

Comments: Insects are trapped and digested by these plants. This process provides additional nitrogen to the plant to help supplement its growth in nitrogen-poor habitats. This added nitrogen may also aid in more robust flower formation. Once the insect becomes trapped on the sticky hairs of the leaf, digestive enzymes are released and the entire process can take up to a week to complete. There are several other species of sundews that occur in the New England region. Thread-Leaved Sundew (*D. filiformis*) has leaves that are long and linear and is found in scattered sites in southern Connecticut, Rhode Island, and western Massachusetts. Round-Leaved Sundew (*D. rotundifolia*), the smallest of the 3 species, has short, round leaves and is common throughout the region.

AUTUMN OLIVE
Elaeagnus umbellata
Autumn-Olive Family (Elaeagnaceae)

Description: This plant is a large, branching shrub, 3–30' tall. The leaves are simple, alternate, lanceolate, 1–5" long, up to 1" wide, and silvery green, with a smooth margin. The shrub produces numerous flowers. Flowers, 1 to several, are found in the leaf axils. The flowers are a creamy yellow color and highly fragrant with a tubular corolla and 4 petals. The flowers produce numerous, juicy red berries.

Bloom Season: May–early June.

Habitat/Range: Open woodlands, floodplains, meadows, fields, roadsides, and open areas. Found scattered throughout the region.

Comments: Autumn and Russian Olive (*E. angustifolia*), both Eurasian species, were brought into the area by wildlife managers.

Russian Olive has narrower leaves, more spines along its stems, and a mealy-textured fruit. The plants were touted as a great cover and food plant for wildlife. The bright red berries of Autumn Olive that appear in the late summer–early autumn are favored by many bird species. The shrub grows quickly and often forms dense stands, effectively crowding out native species. In addition, nitrogen-fixing bacteria are associated with the roots. This microbial partnership results in an alteration of the soil chemistry that, over time, is reflected in a change of the numbers and types of species making up the surrounding plant community. Both shrubs are now considered noxious weeds in New England and efforts are under way to limit and/or eradicate these species from the region.

LEATHERLEAF
Chamaedaphne calyculata
Heath Family (Ericaceae)

Description: Leatherleaf is a small, branching evergreen shrub 1–4' tall. The leaves are alternate, lanceolate, and 1–2" long. The dull green leaves have a leathery texture and are dotted with dry, round scales. One to several flowers are found on one-sided terminal clusters. The flowers are white, nodding, and tubular, with 5 tiny lobes, and measure about ¼".

Bloom Season: April–May.

Habitat/Range: Found along bogs, swamps, and ponds throughout the region.

Comments: Leatherleaf is often the dominant shrub species found in bog environments. It is the only species represented in the genus *Chamaedaphne*.

SPOTTED WINTERGREEN
Chimaphila maculata
Heath Family (Ericaceae)

Description: Plants range from 3–9" tall. The evergreen leaves form a whorl at the base of the plant. Leaves are 1–3" long, slightly ovate to lanceolate, with a broad point and pale white stripes along the veins. Flowers, 2–5, are found in a terminal cluster. Each flower is ½–⅝" wide and nodding. Flowers are white (occasionally pale pink) with 5 rounded, waxy petals.

Bloom Season: Late June–August.

Habitat/Range: Dry woodlands, especially in sandy soils. Commonly found throughout Connecticut, Massachusetts, and Rhode Island and southern portions of Vermont and New Hampshire.

Comments: A native plant easily recognized, even in winter, by its conspicuous white-striped leaves.

CREEPING SNOWBERRY
Gaultheria hispidula
Heath Family (Ericaceae)

Description: A creeping, nonbranching plant, 8–16" long, with a hairy stem. The leaves are simple, alternate, round to elliptic, and ¼–⅜" wide, with a pointed tip and a smooth margin. The leaves have a smooth texture on the upper surface and a hairy texture underneath. The inconspicuous white flowers are bell shaped and up to ⅛", with 4 petals.

Bloom Season: Late May–July.

Habitat/Range: Moist woodlands and bogs, often growing on rotting wood.

Comments: The white berries, which are larger and more conspicuous than the flower, have a wintergreen taste.

WINTERGREEN
Gaultheria procumbens
Heath Family (Ericaceae)

Description: Plants are 2–6" long and creeping. The glossy leaves are simple, alternate, elliptic to ovate, and 1–2" long, with a smooth or slightly toothed margin. The leaves are crowded toward the top of the stem and have a wintergreen smell when crushed. The white flowers, 1–3, are found in leaf axils on erect stems. The flowers are nodding, have a waxy texture, range from ¼–⅜", and are bell shaped with 5 petals.

Bloom Season: Late June–early August.

Habitat/Range: Found in woodlands, especially where there are evergreens, and in sandy soils throughout the region. The plant's presence is often considered an indicator of acidic, nutrient-poor soils.

Comments: The leaves and the bright red berries are edible and have frequently been used as a flavor additive. Folk medicine used a leaf tea to treat a variety of ailments from colds to kidney problems. The essential oil component of the leaves, methyl salicylate, is produced commercially these days and used as wintergreen flavoring in a variety of products. The purified oil by itself is toxic in large quantities.

MOUNTAIN LAUREL
Kalmia latifolia
Heath Family (Ericaceae)

Description: A large shade-tolerant evergreen shrub growing up to 20' in height. The leaves are alternate, simple, narrowly ovate, 3–6" long, short stalked, and leather textured and with a smooth margin. Numerous flowers are located in terminal clusters. Flowers are pinkish white, ¾–1" wide, and saucer shaped with 5 petal-like lobes.

Bloom Season: May–June.

Habitat/Range: Open woodlands and rocky slopes in forests. Common throughout the region.

Comments: Native Americans used a leaf tea as an herbal treatment for heart ailments, syphilis, and inflammation. The plant is toxic. Even honey made from the nectar of this plant's flowers has been reported to be potentially deadly to humans. Mountain Laurel is the state flower of Connecticut.

LABRADOR TEA
Ledum groenlandicum
Heath Family (Ericaceae)

Description: This evergreen shrub is highly branched with hairy twigs and grows to 3' in height. The leaves are simple, alternate, lanceolate, ¾–2" long. The leaves are smooth on the upper surface and densely white-hairy or rust colored underneath. The margin is smooth and curled under. The flowers are on round terminal clusters. They are white, with 5 petals, and measure ⅜–½".

Bloom Season: May–June.

Habitat/Range: Wet shorelines, swamps, and bogs. Found throughout the region except for Rhode Island and eastern Massachusetts.

Comments: Native Americans used a leaf tea to treat a wide variety of ailments, including colds, stomachaches, rheumatism, and scurvy. Clothing made from wool was often colored brown by a dye produced from the plant.

INDIAN-PIPE
Monotropa uniflora
Heath Family (Ericaceae)

Description: An erect plant reaching up to 10" in height. The waxy white stem has a translucent quality that gives it a sickly ghostlike appearance. The stem turns dark brown to black in autumn. Leaves are reduced to scales that character-istically blacken with age. Each stem sports a solitary terminal white (or sometimes pink) flower, ¼–1" long. Flowers are nodding, urn shaped, with 4–5 overlapping oblong petals and 10–12 stamen and 1 pistil.

Bloom Season: July–early October.

Habitat/Range: Found in rich, shady woodlands. This plant is common throughout the region.

Comments: Devoid of chlorophyll, this saprophyte derives its nutrients from a fungal relationship that is associated with its root system. The plants were used by Native Americans to treat sore eyes and colds. The dried roots were used by early physicians to treat nervous disorders and fainting.

ROUNDED SHINLEAF

Pyrola americana

Heath Family (Ericaceae)

Description: Plants are 4–10" tall with dark olive green foliage. The leaves are simple, basal, elliptic or round, 1–3" long, and leather textured, frequently with pale green veins and a smooth margin. The flowers are found on racemes. Flowers are white, nodding, waxy textured, ½–¾". Each flower has 5 rounded petals, 5 green sepals (longer than they are wide), and a protruding style.

Bloom Season: July–August.

Habitat/Range: Woodlands. Found throughout the region.

Comments: Native Americans used the leaves to treat urinary-tract infections. Modern research has shown that the leaves contain arbutin, a glucoside with both antimicrobial and diuretic properties.

COMMON SHINLEAF

Pyrola elliptica

Heath Family (Ericaceae)

Description: Plants, 4–12", with a basal rosette of dark green leaves that are short-stalked, 1–3" long, and elliptic or oblong in shape, with a smooth margin. Flowers are found on racemes. The flowers are white, nodding, and ⅜–½" wide, with 5 greenish-veined petals and a conspicuous, curved protruding style.

Bloom Season: June–August.

Habitat/Range: Dry woodlands. Found throughout the region.

Comments: Native Americans sought to alleviate sore throats by gargling with a tea made from the leaves and drank a root tea as a general health tonic.

SWAMP HONEYSUCKLE
Rhododendron viscosum
Heath Family (Ericaceae)

Description: A medium-sized shrub, 3–8',
branched, and with hairy twigs. The leaves are
simple, opposite, narrowly ovate, and 1–3" long.
The upper surface of each leaf is glossy green,
contrasted with a whitish lower surface. The
flowers are found in clusters. They are white,
1½–2" long, and 5 lobed, with reddish sticky
hairs. Five long, curved stamens and 1 even
longer style protrude out of the corolla.

Bloom Season: June–August.

Habitat/Range: Mainly found in swamps in
Connecticut, Rhode Island, and Massachusetts.

Comments: This species is considered rare in
Vermont, New Hampshire, and Maine, which are
at the northern limits of its range.

MEADOWSWEET
Spiraea alba
Heath Family (Ericaceae)

Description: A small woody shrub, 2–6' tall. The
leaves are alternate, simple, oblong to ovate,
broader at the tip, and 1–2½" long, and with a
smooth margin. Numerous white to pale pink
flowers are borne on panicles 3–5" high. Each
flower measures ⅛–¼" wide and has 5 petals and
5 sepals.

Bloom Season: June–September.

Habitat/Range: Old fields, meadows, swamps,
and shorelines throughout the region.

Comments: Native Americans used the leaves
and flowers of Meadowsweet for medicinal
purposes similar to other species of *Spiraea* such
as Hardhack (*Spiraea tomentosa*).

LOWBUSH BLUEBERRY
Vaccinium angustifolium
Heath Family (Ericaceae)

Description: This low shrub usually does not exceed 2' in height. The sessile leaves are lanceolate and less than 1¼" long, with a minutely toothed margin and a smooth textured upper and lower surface. The flowers are white to pinkish white, ¼" long, and bell shaped with 5 lobes. A few are found in terminal clusters.

Bloom Season: May–June.

Habitat/Range: Dry woodlands with sandy or acidic soils. Common throughout the region.

Comments: This native shrub produces a very tasty fruit and one that is an important food resource for wildlife. Native Americans brewed up a leaf tea that was used as a blood purifier and a treatment for colic and labor pains.

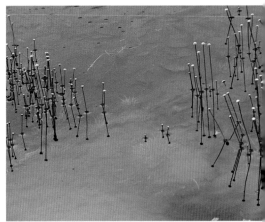

HIGHBUSH BLUEBERRY
Vaccinium corymbosum
Heath Family (Ericaceae)

Description: This plant is a tall-growing (up to 10'), highly branched shrub with green or red twigs. The green leaves are narrowly ovate, 1–3" long, smooth on the topside, and slightly hairy underneath, with a smooth margin. The flowers are white, ¼–½" long, and bell shaped and found in terminal clusters.

Bloom Season: May.

Habitat/Range: Found in woodlands and swamps throughout the region.

Comments: This native shrub serves as an important food resource for wildlife in the region. All cultivated blueberries were derived from this species. Species of blueberry can be found growing on nearly every continent. Only in North America, however, is the plant grown as a crop. Although Highbush Blueberry is the main commercially grown cultivar, Lowbush Blueberry is also marketed in New England.

PIPEWORT
Eriocaulon aquaticum
Pipewort Family (Eriocaulaceae)

Description: These plants are 3–8" and are often found submerged in shallow, standing water. The leaves are basal and grasslike with pointed tips and are up to 4" long. The solitary white flower head is round and about ½" in diameter and sits on top of a stalk that is 5–7 ribbed and leafless. The head is composed of numerous tiny flowers.

Bloom Season: July–early October.

Habitat/Range: Shallow water areas, pond and lake shorelines, and bogs. Found throughout the region.

Comments: *E. aquaticum* is the most common of several pipewort species found in New England.

HOG PEANUT
Amphicarpaea bracteata
Bean Family (Fabaceae)

Description: Hog Peanut is a climbing vine that can reach 6' in length and is slightly hairy. Leaves are divided into 3 leaflets. Each leaflet is ovate, ¾–3" long, rounded at the base, and pointed at the tip and with a smooth margin. Two types of flowers are found on racemes that arise from the leaf axils. The upper flowers are white to pale lavender, nodding, pea-like, to ½". The lower flowers are smaller and lack petals.

Bloom Season: July–August.

Habitat/Range: Woodlands and thickets. Common throughout the region.

Comments: The roots were boiled and eaten by Native Americans. Occasionally the roots were used to treat stomach problems.

ROUND-HEADED BUSH CLOVER
Lespedeza capitata
Bean Family (Fabaceae)

Description: Erect plants, 2–4' tall. The leaves are divided, cloverlike, with 3 leaflets. Each leaflet is elliptic, 1–1½" long, hairy, and short stalked (about ⅛") with a smooth margin. The flowers are found in numerous round heads that arise from the leaf axils. Each head measures about 1–1¼" across. The flowers are white with reddish spots and are about ⅜" long.

Bloom Season: Late June–early September.

Habitat/Range: Open woodlands, dry fields, and sandy soils. Found throughout the region to central Maine.

Comments: As is the case with other legumes, the roots of *L. capitata* are able to fix nitrogen. The seeds are a food source for a number of bird and mammal species.

WHITE SWEET CLOVER
Melilotus alba
Bean Family *(Fabaceae)*

Description: Plants are loosely branched and 2–8' tall. The leaves are alternate, compound, divided into 3 leaflets. The leaflets are elliptic to oval, broader at either end, ½–1" long, with a toothed margin. Numerous fragrant white flowers are found on tall slender racemes arising from the leaf axils. Each raceme measures 2–8". The pea-like flowers (⅛–¼") have 5 united petals and 5 united sepals.

Bloom Season: June–October.

Habitat/Range: Fields, waste areas, and roadsides. Found throughout the area.

Comments: A native of Eurasia, this plant was widely planted to help enrich soil nitrogen in pasturelands. The plants contain coumarin, which has been reported to be toxic to a variety of livestock. A commercially produced and highly prized honey is made mainly from the nectar of White Sweet Clover and Alfalfa.

WHITE CLOVER
Trifolium repens
Bean Family (Fabaceae)

Description: These creeping plants grow 4–12" long. The leaves are on separate stalks than the flowers. The leaves are alternate and compound with 3 leaflets. Each leaflet is ovate, ½–¾", with a notched base and a finely toothed margin. The leaves are green with a paler green "V" marking. The white to pinkish white flowers are found on round heads in terminal clusters that are stalked and up to 1½" wide.

Bloom Season: May–October.

Habitat/Range: Roadsides, fields, and lawns. Commonly found throughout the region.

Comments: White Clover was originally introduced from Europe as a forage crop. The plant can form large colonies due to its ability to root at the nodes. Native Americans brewed a tea from the leaves to treat fevers and colds. Europeans made a tea from the flower that was used to help combat rheumatism.

STAR OF BETHLEHEM
Ornithogalum umbellatum
Hyacinth Family (Hyacinthaceae)

Description: Plants emerge from bulbs and average 6–10" in height. The dark green leaves are linear, 6–10" long, with a smooth margin that curves inward. Flowers, usually 3–8, are found on flat-topped racemes. The white flowers are 1" wide and star shaped with 6 petals that are narrowly ovate and have green striping on the underside. The flowers open around midday and close in the evening.

Bloom Season: May–early July.

Habitat/Range: Lawns, disturbed areas, roadsides, open woodland, meadows, and fields. Found from the southern parts of the region into central Vermont and New Hampshire.

Comments: A garden escape originally introduced from Europe. The plant produces bulbs at a rapid rate, often crowding out other species. Once established the plant is difficult to eradicate. Caution: The bulbs and leaves are extremely poisonous!

HEMP NETTLE
Galeopsis tetrahit
Mint Family (Lamiaceae)

Description: Plants are hairy, 6–30" tall, and square stemmed. The leaves are simple, opposite, ovate to elliptic, 1–4" long, stalked, and hairy with a toothed margin. The white to occasionally pink flowers are on terminal or axillary clusters. The corolla is tube shaped. The 5-lobed calyx is hairy and up to ¾" long.

Bloom Season: July–August.

Habitat/Range: Fields, weedy areas, and roadsides. Found throughout the region.

Comments: Introduced from Eurasia. Flowers from North American plants are generally white in color while those found in Europe are pink.

AMERICAN BUGLEWEED

Lycopus americanus
Mint Family (Lamiaceae)

Description: Plants are hairless, 6–24" tall, with a square stem. The leaves are simple, opposite, lanceolate, 2–4" long, short stalked, and coarsely toothed with a pointed tip. The flowers are found in axillary whorls. The white tubular flowers are ⅛" with 4 petals and 5 narrowly triangular sepals that are shorter than the petals.

Bloom Season: July–August.

Habitat/Range: Moist soils, especially near water. Found throughout the region.

Comments: Whole plants were used as a treatment for coughs.

WILD MINT

Mentha arvensis
Mint Family (Lamiaceae)

Description: Plants are 6–24" tall with a square stem. The leaves are simple, opposite, narrowly ovate to lanceolate, ¾–2" long, and aromatic, with a toothed margin. Numerous flowers are found in clusters at the nodes. The flower clusters encircle the stem. Flowers can be white, pale lavender, or pale pink. Each flower is ⅛" wide and ¼" long and bell shaped.

Bloom Season: July–September.

Habitat/Range: Found along streams and moist places throughout the region.

Comments: Native Americans used a leaf tea to help reduce fevers, sore throats, gas, indigestion, and diarrhea. While there is a mix of native and nonnative species in North America, *M. arvensis* is the only native mint species found in New England.

HOARY MOUNTAIN MINT

Pycnanthemum incanum
Mint Family (Lamiaceae)

Description: Plants are 1–3' tall and hairy. The leaves are simple, opposite, elliptic or ovate, 1–4" long, and hairy. Numerous flowers are in rounded clusters arising from the leaf axils and from the top of the stem. The white flowers are ¼" long and 2 lobed, with a hairy calyx and whitish bracts beneath the flower clusters.

Bloom Season: July–September.

Habitat/Range: Woodlands and thickets. Found in Connecticut, Rhode Island, and Massachusetts to southern New Hampshire and Vermont.

Comments: A leaf tea was used in folk medicine to treat stomach cramps, colds, and coughs and to reduce fevers.

NARROW-LEAVED MOUNTAIN MINT

Pycnanthemum tenuifolium
Mint Family (Lamiaceae)

Description: Erect plants, 1–3' tall, square-stemmed and hairless or minutely hairy. The leaves are linear, 1–2½" long, sessile, and hairless with a smooth margin. The flowers are located in small dense heads. Individual flowers are tiny, measuring about ⅛", and are white to pale purple with dark purple spots. Calyx is hairy.

Bloom Season: July–August.

Habitat/Range: Woodlands and thickets. Found throughout the region to southern Maine.

Comments: The long thin leaves are characteristic of this member of the Mint Family.

NODDING TRILLIUM
Trillium cernuum
Bunchflower Family (Melanthiaceae)

Description: Nodding Trillium is similar in size to other trillium species, ranging from 8–20". The leaves are found in a whorl of 3. Each leaf is ovate to diamond shaped, and pointed, with smooth margins, and measures 2–4" long. The solitary white flower (1–2" wide) droops down below the leaves from a 1–2" long stalk. The 3 petals are ovate to round in shape and recurved. The anthers are intense pink in color.

Bloom Season: May–June.

Habitat/Range: Moist or wet woodlands. Found throughout the region.

Comments: Trilliums in general do not produce true leaves or stems. The "leaves" are in reality bracts subtending the flower. These bracts have a structure similar to that of leaves and also function in photosynthesis and so are often referred to as leaves in many field guides. The flowering trillium is actually a scape.

LARGE WHITE TRILLIUM
Trillium grandiflorum
Bunchflower Family (Melanthiaceae)

Description: Plants obtain a height of 6–18". The leaves are in a whorl of 3 around the base of the stem. The leaves are 3–4" long, sessile, pointed at the tip, and ovate to round in shape, with a smooth margin. A solitary white flower is borne on the end of a 2–3" long erect stalk. Each flower has 3 elliptic to ovate petals, each with a pointed tip. The erect petals measure 2–4" long and often turn pink with age. There are also 3 narrow green sepals.

Bloom Season: May–early June.

Habitat/Range: Rich, moist woodlands, especially in soils with neutral or alkaline pH. Found in Massachusetts, Vermont, western New Hampshire, and northern Connecticut.

Comments: This species produces the largest flowers of all the trilliums. The plant usually requires at least 5 or 6 growing seasons before producing the first flower.

PAINTED TRILLIUM
Trillium undulatum
Bunchflower Family (Melanthiaceae)

Description: The plants are 8–20" tall with leaves that are found in a whorl of 3. Each leaf is 2–5" long, ovate in shape, short stalked (less than 1"), and sharply pointed with a smooth margin. The solitary flower sits erect on a 1–2" stalk. Flowers measure 2–2½" wide and consist of 3 lanceolate to narrowly ovate petals and 3 green sepals. The petals are white with red-violet veins that are most conspicuous at the base and have a waxy texture.

Bloom Season: May–early June.

Habitat/Range: Moist woodlands, especially those with acidic soils, swamps, and stream banks. Found throughout the region.

Comments: Some pregnant Native American women wishing to stimulate uterine contractions and help speed up delivery ate the flowers, leaves, and sepals of Painted Trillium.

STARFLOWER
Trientalis borealis
Myrsine Family (Myrsinaceae)

Description: These small, erect plants are 3–10"
tall and have a single irregular whorl of 5–9
leaves positioned near the top of the stem. Each
leaf is narrowly ovate, 1–4" long, and pointed at
the tip with a minutely toothed margin. Delicate
stalks arise from leaf axils and are topped with 1
to several white flowers. Each flower is ¼–½"
wide with 7 petals and gold-colored anthers.

Bloom Season: May–early June.

Habitat/Range: Rich woodlands, swamps, and
bogs throughout the range.

Comments: One of the more common woodland
wildflowers growing in New England. This
species is encountered in both deciduous and
coniferous forests.

COMMON WATER LILY
Nymphaea odorata
Water-Lily Family (Nymphaeaceae)

Description: An aquatic plant with large floating
leaves. The plant can grow down to a depth of
15'. The round leaves measure 2–12" wide, with
a deep cleft at the base and smooth margins.
Each leaf is green, above and purplish below.
Flowers are solitary, white or occasionally pink,
and highly fragrant. The flowers rest at or just
above the surface of the water and
characteristically open in the morning and close
by early afternoon. Each flower measures 2–6"
wide with many oblong petals, each 1–4" long.
Numerous yellow stamens are clearly visible.
There are also 4 green sepals present.

Bloom Season: June–early September.

Habitat/Range: Lakes, ponds, and slow-moving
streams and rivers. Found throughout the region.

Comments: Native Americans were known to
make a tea from the large fleshy roots to treat
coughs and mouth sores. Seeds were used as a
foodstuff and were ground for flour. In New
England it is a highly prized food for a number of
mammals including beaver, muskrat, porcupine,
white-tailed deer, and moose.

COMMON ENCHANTER'S NIGHTSHADE

Circaea lutetiana
Evening-Primrose Family (Onagraceae)

Description: The plants measure 6–24". The dark green leaves are simple, opposite, oblong to ovate, and 2–5" long, with a pointed tip and a minutely toothed margin. The leaves decrease in size as they ascend the stem towards the flower cluster. Flowers are on racemes 3–9" tall. Individual flowers are up to ¼" long with 2 white rounded petals that are notched and 2 recurved sepals.

Bloom Season: July–August.

Habitat/Range: Moist woodlands throughout the region.

Comments: This woodland species blooms in the summer and is found mainly in shaded areas.

EASTERN WILLOW-HERB

Epilobium coloratum
Evening-Primrose Family (Onagraceae)

Description: A branching, erect plant 1–2' tall, with fine hairs and a stem frequently purple in color. The leaves are simple, alternate, narrowly ovate, 1–6" long, short stalked, and purple tinged, with a pointed tip and toothed margin. The solitary flower is borne in the upper leaf axils and is white or pink in color, ¼", and frequently nodding, with 4 sepals and 4 notched petals.

Bloom Season: July–August.

Habitat/Range: Wet thickets, swamps, and shorelines. Found throughout the region to southeastern Maine.

Comments: American Marsh Willow-Herb (*E. leptophyllum*) can also be found in the region and has similar-appearing flowers to *E. coloratum* but has leaves that are strongly linear in shape and found in axillary clusters.

DOWNY RATTLESNAKE PLANTAIN
Goodyera pubescens
Orchid Family (Orchidaceae)

Description: This member of the orchid family grows 6–18" in height and has a woolly texture. The dark blue-green leaves are basal, simple, ovate or elliptic, 1–3" long, and white veined with a smooth margin. The flowers are found on 2–8" tall racemes. Each is ¼–⅜", with the 2 upper petals and 2 upper sepals forming a hood. The sepals and petals are essentially identical in color. The lip petal is somewhat cupped.

Bloom Season: Late May–early September.

Habitat/Range: Woodlands, favoring those with acidic soils. It is found throughout the region to southern Maine.

Comments: The species is more prevalent in the southern portion of New England. The common name is derived from the checkered pattern formed from the white veins that superficially resembles snakeskin. This characteristic led Native Americans to use a root tea to treat snakebites.

NODDING LADY'S TRESSES
Spiranthes cernua
Orchid Family (Orchidaceae)

Description: This orchid, considered the most abundant orchid in New England, grows 6–20" tall. The basal leaves are pale green, ovate or narrowly ovate, and up to 10" long, with a smooth margin. The upper leaves on the stem are reduced to scales. Numerous fragrant white flowers are found on hairy spikes. The flowers are set in 3 or 4 rows that characteristically spiral around the spike. Each flower is ½–1" long and arching in a down-turned fashion. The petals are ¼–½" long and linear to narrowly ovate. The 2 lip petals are up to ⅜" long, somewhat ovate, and wavy with a yellow center.

Bloom Season: August–September.

Habitat/Range: Fields, meadows, moist thickets, and disturbed areas throughout the region.

Comments: Native Americans prepared a plant tea to act as a diuretic and to treat urinary-tract infections and venereal disease.

COW-WHEAT
Melampyrum lineare
Broom-Rape Family (Orobanchaceae)

Description: Plants are erect, 4–18" tall. The leaves are simple, opposite, spoon shaped, and up to 2½" long, with a smooth margin. The leaves below the flowers are narrower, almost linear. The flowers are found in pairs in the upper axils. Each flower is about ½" long, tube shaped, short stalked, and 2 lipped. The upper lip is white and 2 lobed. The lower lip is yellow and 3 lobed.

Bloom Season: June–July.

Habitat/Range: Woodlands. Found throughout the region.

Comments: Cow-Wheat is hemi-parasitic on the roots of a number of other plants.

CANCER-ROOT
Orobanche uniflora
Broom-Rape Family (Orobanchaceae)

Description: This parasitic plant grows 3–6" high and is covered in fine hairs. The solitary flowers are on leafless stalks. The stalks arise from a short underground stem. The flowers are upright to curved, ½–1" long, and white or pale violet, with 5 fused petals ending with sharply pointed lobes. The lower 3 lobes are yellow striped.

Bloom Season: May–early July.

Habitat/Range: Moist woodlands, thickets, and fields. Common throughout the region.

Comments: This native plant is parasitic and obtains nutrients from the roots of numerous other species.

NORTHERN WOOD SORREL
Oxalis acetosella
Wood-Sorrel Family (Oxalidaceae)

Description: These are low-growing (2–6") plants with cloverlike leaves. The leaves are basal, compound, and divided into 3 leaflets, each being heart shaped with a smooth margin. The leaflets characteristically fold up at night. The flowers are white to a pinkish white and marked with deep pink veins. The solitary flowers are in the leaf axils and are ½–¾" wide with 5 rounded petals that are notched.

Bloom Season: May–July.

Habitat/Range: Moist woodlands. Found throughout Vermont, New Hampshire, and Maine to western Massachusetts.

Comments: The leaves are edible and have been used sparingly in salads. The high oxalic acid content imparts a mildly sour taste to the leaves.

DUTCHMAN'S BREECHES
Dicentra cucullaria
Poppy Family (Papaveraceae)

Description: The plants grow 6–12" tall. The leaves are basal, long-stalked, compound, and 3–6" long. Each gray-green leaf, triangular in shape, is highly dissected into long narrow segments. The flowers, nodding, are on elongated terminal racemes. The flowers are white with golden-yellow tips measuring ¾" wide. There are 4 petals. The outer 2 petals are long spurred. The combination of the 4 petals gives the flower a roughly V-shaped appearance.

Bloom Season: Mid-April–early May.

Habitat/Range: Rich woodlands. Found throughout most of the region.

Comments: In folk medicine a root tea was employed as a diuretic and a leaf poultice and was used as a remedy for treating a variety of skin ailments.

BLOODROOT
Sanguinaria canadensis
Poppy Family (Papaveraceae)

Description: These plants emerge in the early spring and reach a height of 4–12". A single basal leaf is present. The leaf is initially wrapped around the flowering stem. The bluish green leaf is round, 3–9 lobed, and coarsely toothed and measures 3–8" long. The terminal solitary flower is white and 1–2" wide, with 8–12 oblong petals. The flower possesses numerous stamens creating a golden-orange center. The flowers open at midday and are closed by evening. Each flower lasts only 1 or 2 days. The root has a characteristic orange-red sap.

Bloom Season: April–beginning of May.

Habitat/Range: Rich woodlands. Bloodroot is found throughout New England.

Comments: Native Americans used the root sap as both a dye and insect repellant. In addition, a tea was derived from the root and used to reduce fevers and to treat various lung ailments and rheumatism. Caution: This plant is highly toxic and should never be ingested. The main toxic component is the alkaloid sanguinarine.

POKEWEED
Phytolacca americana
Pokeweed Family (Phytolaccaceae)

Description: A large, branching plant reaching 3–10' in height. The smooth stem is purple-green or reddish in color. The large green leaves are simple, alternate, elliptic in shape, with a smooth margin. Leaves measure 4–12" long and are stalked. Stalks measure ½–2" long. Numerous flowers are borne on long white or pink racemes. The individual flowers are white or pink with a green center and measure ¼".

Bloom Season: July–August.

Habitat/Range: Meadows, fields, roadsides, and damp woodlands. Found throughout the region to southern Maine.

Comments: The large, dark purple berries are highly conspicuous in the late summer and fall.

Fresh leaves and roots, as well as the berries, are poisonous to humans as well as toxic to pigs, sheep, horses, and cattle. The plant's toxic nature is presumed to be due to a combination of saponins, oxalic acid, and the plant alkaloid phytolaccin. Birds and wild mammals, on the other hand, appear to be unaffected by this mix. The early colonists used the sap of the berries as a dye and also as ink. According to European folklore, a tea made from the berries acted as an effective agent for driving out evil spirits from an afflicted individual. Native Americans made a tea from the berries for the treatment of rheumatism and arthritis.

WHITE TURTLEHEAD
Chelone glabra
Plantain Family (Plantaginaceae)

Description: Plants grow up to 3' high. The leaves are simple, opposite, and linear or narrowly ovate, with a pointed tip and toothed margin. The leaves are 2–6" long and sessile or very short stalked. The flowers appear in dense clusters on 1–3" tall spikes. The flowers are white or white with a tinge of pink. Individual flowers measure 1–1½" and are tube shaped and 2 lipped. The upper lip is large, hoodlike, and strongly arching. The lower lip is 3 lobed. The overall appearance of the flower is said to resemble a turtle's head.

Bloom Season: Mid-July–early September.

Habitat/Range: Wet thickets, shorelines, swamps, and marshes. Found throughout the region.

Comments: From the flowers Native Americans made a tea used to combat worms and as a contraceptive. A tea prepared from the leaves was believed to act as an appetite stimulant and laxative and to treat jaundice and liver ailments.

TALL BEARD-TONGUE
Penstemon digitalis
Plantain Family (Plantaginaceae)

Description: The plants are 2–4' tall and erect. The basal leaves are opposite, simple, sessile, and ovate or elliptic. The stem leaves are narrowly ovate and 2–8" long, with a toothed or smooth margin. The flowers are on panicles 4–10" tall and usually sticky. The flowers are white, ½–1¼" long, and stalked. The corolla tube is hairy and swollen in the middle. A series of fine purple lines marks the inside. The small calyx has 5 pointed lobes.

Bloom Season: June–early July.

Habitat/Range: Fields, meadows, and moist, open woodlands. Found throughout the region.

Comments: A similar-looking species found in similar habitats in the region is Eastern White Beard Tongue (*P. pallidus*). The corolla tube of this species is not swollen.

ENGLISH PLANTAIN
Plantago lanceolata
Plantain Family (Plantaginaceae)

Description: Also called Ribgrass or Narrow-Leaved Plantain, this species can reach a height of 20". The basal leaves are simple, lanceolate, deeply ribbed, and dark green in color with a smooth margin. Flowers are on spikes 1–4" tall. Individual flowers are round or cylindrical and greenish white and measure about ⅛" wide.

Bloom Season: May–September.

Habitat/Range: Waste areas, fields, and lawns. Commonly found throughout New England.

Comments: This European introduction has naturalized throughout the region. A tea made from the plant's leaves was traditionally used to treat upper respiratory tract ailments such as coughs and bronchitis.

COMMON PLANTAIN
Plantago major
Plantain Family (Plantaginaceae)

Description: Plants range from 6–18" with blue-green leaves that are simple, basal, and waxy with 3–5 ribs and a smooth margin. They are broadly ovate and can measure up to 8" in length. Numerous, tiny, greenish white flowers are grouped on a slender spike rising from the leaves. Individual flowers measure a mere ¹⁄₁₆" in diameter. Flowers are wind pollinated, and their pollen contributes to many hay-fever allergies.

Bloom Season: April–October.

Habitat/Range: Waste areas, roadsides, fields, and lawns. Common throughout the region.

Comments: Early settlers introduced this species from Europe. Native Americans who believed that the plant appeared wherever the white man traveled nicknamed it "white man's foot." The plant has been widely used in folk medicine around the world. Common Plantain is also rich in beta-carotenes, ascorbic acid, potassium, and calcium.

CULVER'S ROOT
Veronicastrum virginicum
Plantain Family (Plantaginaceae)

Description: Plants grow 2–6' tall, with an erect, hairless stem. The leaves are simple, most commonly found in whorls of 3–7, each 1–5" long and short stalked, with a pointed tip with a toothed margin. The flowers are found on several dense erect spikes, 3–8" tall. The flowers can range from the usual white to a pale purple. Each flower is about ⅜" long and tube shaped with 4 petals and 4 sepals.

Bloom Season: July–August.

Habitat/Range: Woodlands, meadows, thickets, and roadsides. Found in Connecticut, western Rhode Island, central to western Massachusetts to central Vermont, southwestern New Hampshire, and extreme southeastern Maine.

Comments: Native Americans prepared a tea from the dried roots that acted as a very strong laxative. There is some evidence to suggest that the plant may be toxic.

FRINGED BINDWEED
Polygonum cilinode
Smartweed Family (Polygonaceae)

Description: A climbing vine that can reach 6' in length with a stem that is often reddish in color. The widely spaced leaves are ovate to triangular in shape, 2–5" long, notched at the base, and pointed at the tip. At the base of the leaf sheath are reflexed bristles. The flowers form on loose spikes that are 1–4" tall. The flowers are usually white or may be pink tinged. They are small, no greater than ⅛", with 5 petal-like lobes.

Bloom Season: July–August.

Habitat/Range: Woodland edges, including rocky areas and thickets. Found throughout the region.

Comments: Climbing False Buckwheat (*P. scandens*) is very similar in appearance but can be differentiated by the absence of bristles on the leaf sheath and by the long-stalked leaves.

JAPANESE KNOTWEED
Polygonum cuspidatum
Smartweed Family (Polygonaceae)

Description: Fast-growing plants, reaching up to 10' tall and possessing a stout, hollow grayish green stem that is smooth and jointed, with strongly arching branches. The overall appearance is faintly bamboolike. The leaves are alternate, simple, ovate, and 2–6" long with a pointed tip and a smooth margin. Numerous greenish white flowers are on 2–5" long erect clusters that arise from leaf axils. Each flower is ⅛" with 5 petal-like lobes (petals are absent) and 5 sepals. Male and female flowers are on separate plants.

Bloom Season: August–September.

Habitat/Range: Fields, thickets, roadsides, and weedy areas. Found throughout the region.

Comments: Introduced from Asia and brought over to North America as an ornamental. It has since escaped cultivation and is rapidly naturalizing. The stems grow back each year from underground rhizomes that have been reported to reach up to 60' in length. This plant can withstand a wide range of adverse environmental conditions and can spread rapidly, forming dense stands that block out native species. Once this plant has established itself in a given locale, it can be extremely difficult to eradicate.

MILD WATER-PEPPER
Polygonum hydropiperoides
Smartweed Family (Polygonaceae)

Description: Plants are 6–36" tall. The leaves are elliptic to linear, 2–5" long, with leaf sheaths that are short hairy with bristles averaging less than ¼" long. The flowers are found on 1–3" tall spikes, are white and ¼" wide, and have 5 petals.

Bloom Season: August–early October.

Habitat/Range: Grows along marshes and in other shallow water environments. Found throughout the region.

Comments: The plant was used in Asian, European, and North American folk medicine. Caution: Plants of the Smartweed Family can cause skin irritations in sensitive individuals.

DOTTED SMARTWEED
Polygonum punctatum
Smartweed Family (Polygonaceae)

Description: A smooth-stemmed plant, 1–3' tall. The leaves are simple, alternate, narrowly ovate or elliptic, 1–4" long, short stalked, and hairless, with a pointed tip and a smooth margin. The leaf sheaths may be hairless or fringed. The flowers are on 2–6" tall spikes. The flowers display an interrupted growth pattern along the spike. Each flower is white, ⅛", with 5 petals and a green calyx.

Bloom Season: July–August.

Habitat/Range: Found in wet areas, swamps, and shallow waters throughout the region.

Comments: Native Americans used the leaves and flowers to treat stomach pains.

ARROW-LEAVED TEARTHUMB
Polygonum sagittatum
Smartweed Family (Polygonaceae)

Description: Branching plants, 2–5' long, erect or spreading, with a barbed stem. The widely spaced leaves are simple, alternate, generally arrow-shaped, and 1–4" long, with barbed leaf stalks and a smooth margin. The lower leaves have downward-pointing basal lobes. The flowers are on small round spikes found at the ends of branches and the base of the leafstalks. The color ranges from white to the occasional pink. Each has 5 petal-like sepals and is about ⅛" wide.

Bloom Season: July–early October.

Habitat/Range: Marshes, wet fields, and moist meadows. Found throughout the region.

Comments: Halbred-Leaved Tearthumb (*P. arifolium*) is similar in appearance and distribution. It can be differentiated from *P. sagittum* in having larger barbs and flowers with 4 petal-like sepals.

Photo by Henry Wolcott

FEATHERFOIL
Hottonia inflata
Primrose Family (Primulaceae)

Description: Aquatic plants that grow up to 18" long. The stalks, often several per plant, are erect, jointed, hollow, and inflated. Each stalk rises about 3–9" above the waterline. The leaves can be alternate, opposite, or whorled and are located clustered at the base of the plant. Each leaf is pinnately divided into numerous linear-shaped lobes that range from ½–2½" long. This leaf arrangement is responsible for the plant's feathery appearance. The flowers are greenish white and found on terminal clusters and around the stem joint. Each flower measures about ⅛" and has 5 tiny white petals and 5 green sepals that are larger than the petals.

Bloom Season: April–early June.

Habitat/Range: Mainly found in swamps, ponds, and shallow, standing water. This plant grows in scattered locations in Connecticut, Rhode Island, and eastern Massachusetts. Rarely encountered in New Hampshire and Maine.

Comments: After appearing at a given site one year, the plant may not reappear in that same location again for a number of years. Why this happens is still a mystery.

WHITE BANEBERRY
Actaea pachypoda
Crowfoot Family (Ranunculaceae)

Description: White Baneberry is an erect plant, 1–2½' tall. The alternate leaves are large (up to 4"), compound, highly divided, hairless underneath, and narrowly ovate with a toothed margin. The white flowers are in a dense, somewhat oblong cluster supported on a thick stalk. Each flower is ¼" wide with 4–10 petals. The fruit is conspicuous in the late summer to early autumn. The berries are shiny white, marked with a black dot, and on a stalk that has turned from green to pinkish red. The appearance of the berries gives rise to the plant's other common name Doll's Eyes.

Bloom Season: May.

Habitat/Range: Rich woodlands and thickets. Found throughout the region.

Comments: All parts of the plant contain a cardiac glycoside with the highest concentrations found in the berries and roots. The ingestion of just a few berries can cause symptoms of nausea and dizziness. The extremely bitter berries are eaten by some birds and mice. Native Americans made a tea from the roots and used it to treat upper respiratory ailments and also to control menstrual irregularities.

RED BANEBERRY
Actaea rubra
Crowfoot Family (Ranunculaceae)

Description: This plant is bushy and erect, measuring 1–3'. The leaves are alternate, compound, and divided into 9–15 leaflets, each with a toothed margin. Numerous flowers are on a round terminal cluster that is short stalked. Each flower is approximately ¼" wide with 4–10 rather inconspicuous petals and numerous threadlike stamen that give the flowers a feathery appearance. Clusters of red berries appear in late summer.

Bloom Season: May.

Habitat/Range: Rich, moist woodlands and thickets. Found throughout the region.

Comments: Native Americans used this plant in a similar fashion to White Baneberry.

WOOD ANEMONE
Anemone quinquefolia
Crowfoot Family (Ranunculaceae)

Description: These delicate plants grow 2–10"
tall. There is a single basal leaf that is stalked.
The compound stem leaves are found in whorls of
3 with 3–5 sharply toothed leaflets. The solitary
white (occasionally pink) flower is borne atop a
slender stem. Each has 5 oblong petal-like sepals
(petals are absent) and measures ½–1". Flowers
are reactive to light, closing at night, and often
are closed even during cloudy days.

Bloom Season: April–May.

Habitat/Range: Moist or wet woodlands and
thickets. Commonly found throughout New
England.

Comments: This is an early spring wildflower
species. The flower will flutter in the slightest of
breezes. This is the characteristic that has
earned it the common nickname of Windflower.
Anemones were known as the "death flower" in
ancient China because of their frequent use at
funerals.

BLACK COHOSH
Cimicifuga racemosa
Crowfoot Family (Ranunculaceae)

Description: An erect plant, 2–7' tall. The leaves
are compound and twice divided into 3s. Each
leaflet is sharply toothed and up to 4" long.
Numerous white flowers are in several very long
and narrow spikes. Each flower is about ½" wide
with 4–5 sepals that drop off as the flower
opens. Petals are absent. The flower has a
feathery appearance due to the presence of
numerous white stamens.

Bloom Season: July–September.

Habitat/Range: Moist, rich woodlands. Mainly
found in western Massachusetts, western
Connecticut, and extreme southeastern Maine.

Comments: The early settlers used the plant to
treat rheumatism and snakebites and to help
reduce fevers. Native Americans treated
menstrual problems and aided childbirth with root
preparations of Black Cohosh. Modern clinical
trials have shown root extracts to be highly
effective in alleviating menopausal symptoms.

VIRGIN'S BOWER
Clematis virginiana
Crowfoot Family (Ranunculaceae)

Description: A climbing vine reaching up to 10' in length. The compound leaves are opposite and divided into 3 leaflets. Each leaflet is ovate and ¾–4" long, with a notched base, a pointed tip, and a sharply toothed margin. The flowers are found in clusters arising from leaf axils. Each flower is white, about ¾" wide, with 4 petal-like sepals. Petals are absent. The male and female flowers are on separate plants.

Bloom Season: Mid-July–August.

Habitat/Range: The edges of fields and woodlands as well as a variety of moist areas. Found throughout the region.

Comments: Sensitive individuals can develop a rather serious dermatitis from handling the plant.

GOLDTHREAD
Coptis trifolia
Crowfoot Family (Ranunculaceae)

Description: Although a mere 2–6" tall, these plants often form dense mats on forest floors. The basal leaves are trifoliate. Each leaflet is ovate, glossy, and evergreen, with either a toothed or scalloped margin. The flowers are solitary with tiny white petals and 4–7 lanceolate, petal-like sepals and bright yellow stamens.

Bloom Season: May.

Habitat/Range: Mossy woodlands, swamps, and bogs. Found throughout the region.

Comments: The name of this plant is derived from its golden yellow underground stem. Both Native Americans and colonists chewed the root or gargled with a root tea preparation to alleviate mouth sores and toothaches. Both of these uses gave rise to another of the plant's common names, Cankerroot. Teas made from leaves and roots were used to treat a variety of ailments from jaundice to stomach cramps. Native populations of Goldthread are at risk from overharvesting.

GOLDENSEAL
Hydrastis canadensis
Crowfoot Family (Ranunculaceae)

Description: Plants can grow up to 14" in height and basically consist of three green leaves—a single long-stalked basal leaf and 2 stem leaves in an alternate arrangement. A highly wrinkled appearance is characteristic for the leaves. Each leaf has 5–9 lobes, prominent veins, and a toothed margin and measures 4–10". A solitary flower is borne on a hairy stalk rising just above the stem leaves. The greenish white flower measures ¼–½" wide and consists of a rounded cluster of stamens that is devoid of petals. The 3 green sepals drop off early in flowering.

Bloom Season: May.

Habitat/Range: Rich woodlands. Rare in the region, limited to a few locales in Connecticut and Vermont.

Comments: A highly prized and sacred medicinal herb used by Native Americans and the colonists to treat numerous ailments. It contains the alkaloid berberine, which modern science has shown to have antibacterial and antifungal properties. It continues to be widely used today despite the fact that it has been shown to be poisonous, severely affecting the mucous membranes. Overcollection in the wild is the primary cause of its rarity in New England forestlands, which is ironic given the fact that the plant can easily be cultivated.

TALL MEADOW RUE
Thalictrum pubescens
Crowfoot Family (Ranunculaceae)

Description: Plant erect, 3–7' tall. The leaves are compound, bluish green, heart shaped to round, either undivided or 2–3 lobed, and ½–2" wide. The lower leaves are stalked and the upper leaves are sessile. Numerous white flowers are found on panicles. Individual flowers are up to ⅜" wide and devoid of petals. Male and female flowers are on the same plant. The male flower is composed of numerous threadlike stamens. The female flowers have 2 pistils and usually a few stamens. The numerous stamens give the flower a feathery, plumelike appearance.

Bloom Season: June–July.

Habitat/Range: Rich woodlands, moist meadows, swamps, and stream banks. Commonly found throughout the region.

Comments: Some Native Americans used the leaves as a spice.

RUE ANEMONE
Thalictrum thalictroides
Crowfoot Family (Ranunculacae)

Description: Rue Anemone is a delicate plant growing 3–10" tall. The leaves are basal and compound, ovate to round, 3 lobed, and stalked with a toothed margin. The leaves grow in whorls below the flowers. The flowers, 3 or more, are white (rarely pink) with 5–10 ovate, petal-like sepals. The flowers are devoid of petals.

Bloom Season: April–May.

Habitat/Range: Open woodlands. Found in the southern portion of the region.

Comments: Native Americans concocted a tea from the tuberous roots that was used to treat both diarrhea and vomiting.

FALSE VIOLET
Dalibarda repens
Rose Family (Rosaceae)

Description: These plants are creeping, 2–4" long. The basal leaves are dark green, simple, heart shaped, 1–2" wide, and minutely hairy on both sides, with a scalloped margin. The solitary flowers arise in the leaf axils. Each is about ¾", white in color, with 5 rounded petals and numerous stamens.

Bloom Season: July–mid-August.

Habitat/Range: Cool moist woodlands and swamps. Found throughout the region.

Comments: Common name is derived from the plant's resemblance to violets.

COMMON STRAWBERRY

Fragaria virginiana
Rose Family (Rosaceae)

Description: These low-growing plants only reach heights of about 6" and readily spread by creeping stolons. The leaves are dark green to blue green and basal with hairy stalks. Each leaf is divided into 3 leaflets that are narrowly ovate and broader towards either end, with a toothed margin. Flowers, several to many, are on panicles. Individual flowers have a yellow center surrounded by 5 rounded white petals.

Bloom Season: Late April–June.

Habitat/Range: Fields, meadows, and open spaces. Common throughout the region.

Comments: Native Americans brewed a leaf tea to treat a wide range of ailments including stomachaches, diarrhea, and sore throats as well as kidney and bladder problems. The cultivated strawberry, *F. ananassa*, is a fertile hybrid derived from the crossing of two wild species: Beach Strawberry (*F. chiloensis*) and *F. virginiana*.

WHITE AVENS

Geum canadense
Rose Family (Rosaceae)

Description: A somewhat spindly plant, 1–3' tall. The basal leaves are alternate, pinnately compound, and divided into 3 leaflets that are ovate and long stalked. The stem leaves are short stalked and narrowly ovate with a toothed margin. The white flowers are on racemes. Each is up to ½" wide, stalked, with 5 rounded petals and 5 sepals that are shorter in length than the petals.

Bloom Season: June–August.

Habitat/Range: Woodlands and some open areas. Found throughout the range.

Comments: Native Americans prepared a love potion from the whole plant.

RED CHOKEBERRY
Pyrus arbutifolia
Rose Family (Rosaceae)

Description: This native plant is a densely branched spreading shrub up to 12' in height. The leaves are 1–3" long, ovate to lanceolate, with a pointed tip and toothed margin. The leaves are smooth and dark green on the upper surface and densely hairy on the underside and significantly lighter in color. The flowers are located in terminal clusters. The flowers are white to pinkish white and ½" wide, on hairy stalks. Individual flowers are composed of 5 rounded petals, numerous stamens, and highly conspicuous black or dark red anthers.

Bloom Season: Mid-May–late June.

Habitat/Range: Thickets, swamps, and open woodlands. Commonly found throughout the region.

Comments: This shrub can readily form dense thickets. Although the bright red berries tend to persist through most of the winter, they appear to have little importance as a food source for wildlife.

MULTIFLORA ROSE
Rosa multiflora
Rose Family (Rosaceae)

Description: These plants form numerous arching stems to 12' that are covered with short, thick, recurved thorns. The leaves are pinnately compound, divided into 5–11 leaflets. Each leaflet is elliptic to ovate and up to 1" long with a toothed margin. Numerous flowers are found in terminal clusters on the arching stems. The white (sometimes pink) flowers are ¾–1" wide, with 5 petals and 5 sepals, and are highly fragrant.

Bloom Season: May–June.

Habitat/Range: Pastures, fields, roadsides, and woodland edges. Found in Connecticut, Rhode Island, and Massachusetts to extreme southern Vermont and up through central New Hampshire.

Comments: This species is an Asian import and is considered a noxious weed in some states. The plants often form dense, impenetrable masses that serve as excellent ground cover for some animal species.

SWAMP DEWBERRY
Rubus hispidus
Rose Family (Rosaceae)

Description: A bristly, trailing plant up to 8' long. The leaves are divided into 3–5 leaflets. Each leaflet is up to 2" long, narrowly ovate, and shiny and with a toothed margin. Several to many white flowers are on racemes. Each flower is ½–¾" wide with 5 petals, 5 sepals, and numerous stamens and pistils.

Bloom Season: June–August.

Habitat/Range: Moist or dry thickets, open woodlands, and clearings. Found throughout the range.

Comments: Native Americans used the juice from the berries as an astringent and to treat dysentery.

BUTTONBUSH
Cephalanthus occidentalis
Madder Family (Rubiaceae)

Description: A medium-sized aquatic shrub, 3–15' tall. The dark green leaves are simple, opposite or whorled, 3–5" long, and oblong with a pointed tip and smooth margin. Numerous flowers are found in terminal spherical clusters, each 1–1½" wide. Individual flowers are white, about ¼" long, and tubular, with 4 pointed lobes and a long style protruding beyond the corolla, giving each cluster a characteristic pincushion appearance.

Bloom Season: July–August.

Habitat/Range: Found along streams, swamps, and ponds throughout the region.

Comments: The inner bark of Buttonbush was chewed by Native Americans to help alleviate toothaches. Also, a bark tea was used to treat a number of ailments. Two toxic and powerful glucosides—cephalanthin and cephalin—have been identified in Buttonbush. If ingested, these glucosides can cause vomiting, convulsions, and even paralysis. Consumption of the plant's foliage has also been reported to be poisonous to livestock.

CLEAVERS
Galium aparine
Madder Family (Rubiaceae)

Description: Rasping and square-stemmed plants, 1–3' long. The leaves are found in whorls of 6–8. Each leaf is narrowly ovate and sessile, with a single prominent vein and recurved prickly hairs. The flower clusters appear in the axils of the upper leaves. Each flower is tiny (⅛") with 4 white petals.

Bloom Season: June–July.

Habitat/Range: Rich woodlands, fields, and thickets. Found in Connecticut, Rhode Island, Massachusetts, and Vermont to southern New Hampshire and Maine.

Comments: An herbal tea was popular in folk medicine as a diuretic and blood purifier. Scurvy was treated with fresh juice from the plant. Young, tender shoots can be boiled and then eaten or added to salads. A coffee substitute was made from ripened seeds that had been ground and roasted.

NORTHERN BEDSTRAW
Galium boreale
Madder Family (Rubiaceae)

Description: A branching plant, 6–30" tall, with a smooth stem. The leaves are characteristically found in whorls of 4. Each leaf is lanceolate to linear, ½–2" long, and sessile with a smooth margin. The flowers are found in branched terminal clusters. Each flower is white, up to ¼", with a 4-lobed corolla. Sepals are absent.

Bloom Season: July–August.

Habitat/Range: Woodland edges, moist meadows, and rocky soils. Found throughout the region.

Comments: *G. boreale* is often found growing in dense patches that can effectively crowd out other species.

WILD MADDER
Galium mollugo
Madder Family (Rubiaceae)

Description: Plants are 1–3' tall and hairy. The leaves are in whorls of 6–8. Each leaf is narrowly ovate to linear, ½–1½" long, with a single vein and with a smooth margin. Numerous flowers are found on terminal or axillary clusters. Flowers are white and ⅛", with 4 petals.

Bloom Season: July–August.

Habitat/Range: Grows mainly in fields and along roadsides. Found throughout the region.

Comments: Naturalized from Europe and quite common in the region.

PARTRIDGE BERRY
Mitchella repens
Madder Family (Rubiaceae)

Description: The plants are creeping, 4–12" long, and often found growing in mats. The evergreen leaves are simple, opposite, round to ovate, ½–1" wide, stalked, and shiny with faint whitish veins and a smooth margin. The white flowers are terminal, found in pairs that are joined at the base. Individual flowers are up to ⅝" long. The corolla is funnel shaped, with 4 spreading lobes, and is fringed on the inside.

Bloom Season: June–July.

Habitat/Range: Common ground cover found in woodlands throughout the region.

Comments: Native Americans used this plant to treat a variety of ailments. The leaves were considered invaluable in the treatment of menstrual problems and childbirth pain. This usage led to Partridge Berry's other common nickname Squaw Vine.

LILY-OF-THE-VALLEY
Convallaria majalis
Ruscus Family (Ruscaceae)

Description: This garden escape measures 3–8".
There are 2–3 ovate leaves. Each leaf is 5–16"
long and dark green in color, with prominent
parallel veins and a smooth margin. The white
fragrant flowers are found on 1-sided racemes.
Individual flowers are bell shaped and nodding
and measure ¼–⅜".

Bloom Season: May–June.

Habitat/Range: Open areas, field edges, and
thickets. Scattered throughout the region to
central Maine.

Comments: Originally a European introduction,
this species has widely escaped cultivation. The
plant spreads by root runners. Flower and root
teas were used in folk medicine to reduce fevers,
to treat epilepsy, and to act as a heart tonic.

CANADA MAYFLOWER
Maianthemum canadense
Ruscus Family (Ruscaceae)

Description: Canada Mayflower often forms
extensive colonies containing numerous small
plants, 2–8" tall. The 2 leaves present on each
plant are ovate to somewhat heart shaped, 1–4"
long, pointed at the tip, and sessile or short
stalked, with a notched base. The dark green
leaves have a glossy sheen to them. Ten to 20
white flowers are found on an erect raceme 1–2"
tall. The flowers are star shaped, ¼", with 4
petal-like parts. Very few individual plants in a
colony flower in any given year.

Bloom Season: May–June.

Habitat/Range: Moist or dry woodlands. One of
the most common wildflowers found throughout
the region.

Comments: Native Americans made both a plant
tea and a root tea to help alleviate headaches
and sore throats respectively. The tiny flowers are
pollinated primarily by native bees and flies.

FALSE SOLOMON'S SEAL
Maianthemum racemosum
Ruscus Family (Ruscaceae)

Description: This plant has an arching stem with a characteristic slight zigzag bend to it, ranges from 1–3' long, and is finely hairy. The sessile leaves are simple, alternate, elliptic, 2–6" long with a pointed or blunt tip, and rounded at the base, with a smooth margin. The leaves are hairy on the underside and conspicuously parallel veined. Numerous white or off-white flowers are borne on 2–6" tall panicles. Individual flowers measure ⅛–¼" with 6 oblong petal-like lobes. The bloom has a feathery appearance.

Bloom Season: May–June.

Habitat/Range: Rich woodlands. Common throughout the region.

Comments: The leaves and roots were used in folk medicine. A root tea preparation was used to combat rheumatism and alleviate constipation. A leaf tea was used to treat coughs and as a contraceptive.

BASTARD TOADFLAX
Comandra umbellata
Sandalwood Family (Santalaceae)

Description: Plants are 6–18" tall. The leaves are alternate, simple, oblong to elliptic, ¾–2" long, with a smooth margin. The white flowers are found on terminal panicles. Each flower is funnel shaped and ⅛" wide with 5 sepals. Petals are absent.

Bloom Season: May–June.

Habitat/Range: Fields and thickets. Found in Connecticut, Massachusetts, Rhode Island, and New Hampshire to southern portions of Vermont and Maine.

Comments: The species is a hemi-parasite. It is photosynthetic but also obtains some nutrients from the roots of other plants.

EARLY SAXIFRAGE
Saxifraga virginiensis
Saxifrage Family (Saxifragaceae)

Description: Early Saxifrage grows up to 12" tall. The green leaves, mostly basal, are simple, ovate, and stalked (up to 3" long), with a slightly toothed margin. Numerous small flowers are borne on a branched terminal cluster. Individual flowers are white with 5 rounded petals and measure approximately ¼".

Bloom Season: Late April–May.

Habitat/Range: Rocky areas, ledges, and moist or dry woodlands. Found throughout the region except for northern Maine.

Comments: In folk medicine, Early Saxifrage was prescribed for the treatment of gallstones.

FOAMFLOWER
Tiarella cordifolia
Saxifrage Family (Saxifragaceae)

Description: Foamflower often forms large colonies with individual plants ranging in size from 4–12". Leaves are simple, basal, often hairy, and somewhat heart shaped, with 3–5 lobes and a toothed margin. Flowers are found in a narrow terminal cluster. Individual flowers are white with 5 petals and 10 very long stamens. The long stamens impart a feathery look to the flower.

Bloom Season: May–June.

Habitat/Range: Woodlands. Found throughout the region with the exception of Rhode Island and eastern Massachusetts.

Comments: A tea was made from the leaves of the plant and used by Native Americans as a mouthwash. Additionally, a tea made from the roots was utilized as a diuretic.

JIMSON WEED
Datura stramonium
Nightshade Family (Solanaceae)

Description: Plants erect, loosely branched, 2–5' tall, often with purplish green stems. The leaves are simple, alternate, narrowly ovate, slightly hairy, and up to 8" long with a coarse and irregular toothed margin faintly resembling that of oaks. Both the leaves and stems give off a rather unpleasant odor when crushed. The flowers are solitary, terminal, and found in the axils. They are white to lavender and up to 3" long with 5 petals and shaped like a funnel. Each petal has a prominent "tooth" at the end. The large fruit (2" wide) is somewhat egg shaped and covered with numerous stiff spines. The flowers usually open around twilight and are pollinated by sphinx moths.

Bloom Season: July–September.

Habitat/Range: Fields, waste areas, and some shorelines. Found throughout Connecticut, Massachusetts, and Rhode Island. The plant is less common in Vermont, New Hampshire, and Maine.

Comments: Jimson Weed's origin is still in question. Some experts believe it was originally from tropical America while others target India. All parts of this plant are poisonous. The seeds, when ingested, produce a narcotic effect and have been responsible for a number of poisonings and even deaths, especially among teenagers. The plants contain a number of alkaloids, the primary ones being atropine, hyoscyamine, and scopolamine. Even handling the leaves or flowers can cause skin irritation in sensitive individuals.

HORSE NETTLE
Solanum carolinense
Nightshade Family (Solanaceae)

Description: A plant 1–3' tall with a stem and leaves that have spiny prickles. The leaves are simple, alternate, ovate, 2–5" long, coarsely toothed or lobed, and very spiny. Several flowers are found in loose racemes. Each flower is white to pale violet with a yellow center and a star-shaped corolla.

Bloom Season: June–October.

Habitat/Range: Fields, meadows, and weedy areas. Found in Connecticut, Rhode Island, and Massachusetts to southern Vermont and New Hampshire.

Comments: Native Americans gargled with a leaf tea to soothe sore throats and very sparingly used the toxic berries to treat a wide range of ailments. The leaves were crushed and applied to poison-ivy rash.

FLOATING BUR-REED
Sparganium fluctuans
Bur-Reed Family (Sparganiaceae)

Description: The floating stems of this aquatic plant can reach up to 5' in length. The leaves are grasslike and also floating and 1–3' long with a smooth margin. Flowers are devoid of sepals and petals and possess a single stigma. Two to 4 heads, white in color, are found on branches that rise 6–10" above the water surface. Each head is approximately ¾" wide.

Bloom Season: July–August.

Habitat/Range: Found in old ponds, lakes, swamps, and shallow water in Maine, Vermont, New Hampshire, Maine, and eastern Massachusetts. It is considered endangered in Connecticut.

Comments: The starchy tubers are edible.

WHITE VERVAIN
Verbena urticifolia
Verbena Family (Verbenaceae)

Description: Plants are erect, 1–5' tall, loosely branched, and hairy. The leaves are ovate to elliptic, 3–6" long, rounded at the base, long stalked, and hairless or nearly so, with a coarsely toothed margin. Flowers are found along erect spikes and may or may not display an interrupted growth pattern. The flowers are white and small, about ¼".

Bloom Season: July–August.

Habitat/Range: Woodland and thicket borders and weedy areas throughout the region.

Comments: This weedy species has a particular fondness for habitats that have been repeatedly disturbed.

TALL WHITE VIOLET
Viola canadensis
Violet Family (Violaceae)

Description: This native member of the Violet Family grows 6–12" tall. The leaves are basal, ovate to heart shaped, and 2–4", with a toothed margin. The solitary flower arises in leaf axils. The white to pale violet flower measures approximately ½" in width, is short stalked, and has 5 petals. The petals are yellow at the base with pale purple backs.

Bloom Season: May–June.

Habitat/Range: Rich woodlands. Found in Vermont, New Hampshire, Massachusetts, and western Connecticut.

Comments: Native Americans prepared a root tea to treat bladder problems. Roots and leaves were used as a traditional folk medicine to induce vomiting.

LANCE-LEAVED VIOLET
Viola lanceolata
Violet Family (Violaceae)

Description: These tiny plants grow 2–5". The leaves are basal, narrowly ovate, 1–4" long, and dark green in color, with a pointed tip, somewhat tapered base, and a smooth margin. The flowers are solitary, white, and ¼–½" in width with 5 petals. The lower petal is marked with purple lines.

Bloom Season: May.

Habitat/Range: Occurs in swamps and pond edges and along stream banks. Found throughout the region.

Comments: The plant can reproduce by seed or from stolons.

WILD WHITE VIOLET
Viola macloskeyi
Violet Family (Violaceae)

Description: These diminutive plants grow 2–5". The leaves can be round or heart shaped, ½–3" long, and deeply notched at the base with a smooth margin. The white flowers are solitary and nodding. Each flower is ¼–½" wide, with 5 green sepals and 5 petals. The lateral petals do not angle forward. The lower 3 petals have a series of fine purple lines marking them.

Bloom Season: May–June.

Habitat/Range: Shaded woodlands and stream banks. Found throughout the region.

Comments: Another species of violet that can reproduce by seed or by stolons.

PINK AND RED FLOWERS

This section includes wildflowers that range from pale pink to maroon to vivid scarlet. These colors can grade into hues of pale purple or white. Those sections should also be checked.

FIELD GARLIC
Allium vineale
Onion Family (Alliaceae)

Description: Field Garlic is an herb, 1–3' tall, that arises from a bulb. The dark green grasslike leaves are simple, alternate, linear, round, and hollow inside, with a pointed tip and a smooth margin. Numerous (up to 50) pinkish purple flowers are found on a terminal umbel. Beneath the cluster is a single bract. Flowers are often replaced by small bulblets with long tails.

Bloom Season: May–early July.

Habitat/Range: Meadows, fields, and pastures. Found in Connecticut, Rhode Island, and Massachusetts to southern Vermont and southern New Hampshire.

Comments: This species is originally from Europe. Imparts a rather strong garlic taste when eaten.

SWAMP MILKWEED

Asclepias incarnata
Dogbane Family (Apocypaceae)

Description: A tall (1–5'), branching plant with a milky sap. The leaves are simple, opposite, oblong or lanceolate, 2–6" long, with a smooth margin. The flowers are in flat terminal clusters. Each cluster measures 1–2" wide and is branched. Each flower is deep pink to magenta, about ⅜" wide, with 5 recurved petals and a 5-pointed crownlike center.

Bloom Season: July–August.

Habitat/Range: Swamps, thickets, marshes, wet meadows, and stream banks throughout the region.

Comments: A tea made from the roots was used as a diuretic and laxative and also used to induce vomiting. The colonists used it to combat asthma, rheumatism, and syphilis. Native Americans made a good-quality cordage from the stem fibers.

COMMON MILKWEED

Asclepias syriaca
Dogbane Family (Apocynaceae)

Description: An erect, stout-stemmed plant, 3–6' tall, with a characteristic milky sap. The leaves are simple, opposite, stalked, and oblong. Each leaf has a prominent midvein and a smooth margin and measures 6–10" in length. The leaves are light green on the upper surface and gray downy on the underside. Numerous highly fragrant flowers are found in 2 or more round, drooping clusters. Each cluster is 2–4" wide with numerous dull pink-purple flowers. Each flower is approximately ⅜", with 5-reflexed petals and a conspicuous center crown with 5 points. Seedlings usually take 2–3 years before producing flowers.

Bloom Season: Late June–July.

Habitat/Range: Fields, meadows, and roadsides. Commonly found throughout the region.

Comments: Native Americans prepared a root tea as a laxative and a diuretic. Early physicians used plant extracts to treat asthma and rheumatism. Milkweeds contain cardiac glycosides. Monarch Butterfly larvae feed almost exclusively on milkweed and concentrate significant amounts of these compounds in their body tissues, which makes the butterfly toxic to many predators. Milkweeds grown in different parts of the country exhibit differing cardiac glycoside profiles. In colonial times seed tassels were frequently used to stuff pillows and mattresses.

PASTURE THISTLE
Cirsium pumilum
Composite Family (Asteraceae)

Description: Small, hairy, thistle plants that reach 1–3' in height. The leaves are lobed, elliptic to oblong, with numerous small spines along the margins of the leaves and a few larger ones scattered over the leaves and stem. The pink flower heads—1 to several are found at the end of the branches—are 2–3" long.

Bloom Season: July–late September.

Habitat/Range: Pastures, fields, and open woodlands. Found throughout the region to southern Maine.

Comments: Unlike other thistle plants, this one is not white woolly.

BULL THISTLE
Cirsium vulgare
Composite Family (Asteraceae)

Description: A branching, spiny-stemmed plant that grows 2–6' tall. The leaves are simple, alternate, lobed, spiny, 3–6" long, and sparsely white-haired underneath. The flower heads, 1–3, are found at the ends of prickly branches. Each flower head measures 1½–2½" wide and is rose-purple in color. The involucral bracts are pointed and tipped with a yellow spine.

Bloom Season: July–August.

Habitat/Range: Fields, pastures, roadsides, and weedy areas. Commonly found throughout the region.

Comments: Originally from Eurasia. This introduced species is often an aggressive colonizer of disturbed habitats.

COMMON FLEABANE
Frigeron philadelphicus
Composite Family (Asteraceae)

Description: Plants are 6–30" tall, spreading, and somewhat hairy. The basal leaves are simple, alternate, elliptic to ovate, up to 6" long, rounded, and lobed or coarsely toothed. The stem leaves are smaller, oblong, and clasping, with a toothed margin. The flower heads are found in terminal and upper axial clusters. The heads measure ½–1" in diameter with a large yellow disk that is surrounded by rays that are pink to white in color. There can be as many as 500 rays present, but only 50–150 are present on average.

Bloom Season: April–August.

Habitat/Range: Weedy places, fields, thickets, and occasionally open woodlands. Found throughout the region.

Comments: The plant was used in folk medicine as a diuretic and to treat diarrhea and urinary tract ailments, as well as a host of other maladies.

SPOTTED JOE-PYE-WEED
Eupatorium maculatum
Composite Family (Asteraceae)

Description: A plant, 2–6' tall, with a sturdy stem that is frequently purple or purple tinged. The leaves are in whorls of 4–5 and are narrowly ovate to elliptic, 2–7" long, and short stalked with a toothed margin. The flower heads are on flat-topped panicles and are pinkish purple and ¼–⅜" long and contain only disk flowers.

Bloom Season: Mid-July–early September.

Habitat/Range: Moist places such as meadows, thickets, and shorelines. Found throughout the region.

Comments: Native Americans used a tea produced from the whole plant as a diuretic. A root tea preparation was used to treat colds, chills, fevers, and liver and kidney ailments.

CARDINAL FLOWER
Lobelia cardinalis
Bellflower Family (Campanulaceae)

Description: An erect plant, 2–4' tall, with a milky sap. The leaves are simple, alternate, lanceolate, with a pointed tip and toothed margin, and measure up to 6" long. The lower leaves are short stalked while the smaller upper leaves are sessile. The flowers are found on racemes, 4–18" tall. The bright scarlet flowers measure 1–1¾" and have a tubular appearance with 5 petal-like lobes. On rare occasions pink or white flowers may occur. The corolla is 2 lipped. The upper lip has 2 lobes; and the lower, 3 lobes. The stamens extend beyond the corolla. A small bract is situated at the base of each flower.

Bloom Season: Mid-July–August.

Habitat/Range: Wet meadows, swamps, along streams and pond edges. Found scattered throughout the region.

Comments: Hummingbirds are the plant's main pollinator. Native Americans made a tea from the root that was used to treat syphilis and typhoid. Colds, fevers, and headaches were treated with a leaf tea. In New England habitat loss and overcollecting are taking a toll on populations of these beautiful and showy wildflowers. The plant contains potentially toxic alkaloids. Colonial farmers in New England believed that cows miscarried after eating the plant.

DEPTFORD PINK
Dianthus ameria
Pink Family (Caryophyllaceae)

Description: Plants are 6–24" tall and hairy. The basal leaves are simple, opposite, elliptic to ovate, 1–3" long, and hairy, with a pointed tip and a smooth margin. Stem leaves are linear. The flowers are in terminal clusters. The flowers are dark pink and hairy, with 5 elliptic to ovate petals that have a toothed margin and numerous tiny white spots. There are also leaflike bracts below the flowers.

Bloom Season: May–August.

Habitat/Range: Fields, weedy areas, and roadsides. Found throughout the area to southern Maine.

Comments: Originally a European introduction.

RAGGED ROBIN
Lychnis flos-cuculi
Pink Family (Caryophyllaceae)

Description: A sparsely hairy plant, 1–2' tall. The basal leaves are simple, opposite, lanceolate, 2–4" long, and short stalked, with a smooth margin. The stem leaves are smaller, narrowly ovate, and sessile. The pink flowers are found on branched panicles. Flowers measure 1" in width with a bell-shaped calyx and 5 petals that are deeply cut, lending a somewhat ragged (hence the common name) look to the flower.

Bloom Season: May–June.

Habitat/Range: Roadsides, fields, and meadows. Found throughout the region.

Comments: This attractive European introduction has become established throughout much of the New England region. It is, however, considered a noxious weed in some states (such as Connecticut).

SHEEP LAUREL
Kalmia angustifolia
Heath Family (Ericaceae)

Description: A small, evergreen shrub rarely exceeding 3' in height. The dark green leaves are in whorls of 3, each 1–2½" long, and oblong, with a smooth margin and a leathery texture. The flowers are in dense clusters around the stem. They are deep pink, saucer shaped, and up to ½" wide, with 5 petals. Most of the flowers are found below the leaves.

Bloom Season: Mid-May–early July.

Habitat/Range: Old fields, swamps, bogs, and sandy soils. Found throughout the region.

Comments: The foliage, when ingested, is highly poisonous to livestock. The toxic component is grayanotoxin (previously call acetylandromedol) and is found to varying levels in all laurels. Native Americans used minute amounts of the leaves in a tea preparation to treat colds and stomach ailments.

BOG LAUREL
Kalmia polifolia
Heath Family (Ericaceae)

Description: A small shrub topping off at about 3'. The leaves are simple, opposite or in whorls of 3, each ½–1½" long, and sessile, with smooth margins that are rolled inward. The upper surface is dark green while the lower surface is white. The flowers arise in the upper axils in loose clusters. Individual flowers are pale pink, ¼–½", and saucer shaped, with 5 lobes.

Bloom Season: May–June.

Habitat/Range: Mainly in bogs and fens. Found throughout the New England region with the exception of Rhode Island.

Comments: All parts of the plant are poisonous due to the presence of grayanotoxin. This compound is also contained in the nectar and can result in a poisonous honey if concentrations are high enough.

PINESAP
Monotropa hypopithys
Heath Family (Ericaceae)

Description: A branchless, reddish pink or yellow plant with a soft hairy stem. The leaves are reduced to tiny, clasping scales. The flowers have the same coloration as the stem. Three to 6 flowers are found on 1-sided racemes. The flowers are nodding and tubular, with 4–5 petals, and measure ¼–½". The plants that flower early in the summer are yellow while those that flower in the autumn are red in color.

Bloom Season: Late July–October.

Habitat/Range: Rich woodlands with acidic soils. Frequently found under oaks and pines. Found throughout the region.

Comments: This non-chlorophyll-containing plant is a saprophyte and obtains its nutrients from fungi that are closely associated with the roots of pines and oaks.

PINK AZALEA
Rhododendron periclymenoides
Heath Family (Ericaceae)

Description: A small, highly branched shrub, 2–6' in height, occasionally topping off at 12'. The green leaves are found in whorl-like clusters at the ends of twigs. Each leaf is 2–4" long, somewhat oblong, with a pointed tip and smooth margin. The pink flowers are found in terminal clusters. Flowers are approximately 1–2" wide and funnel shaped, with a 5-lobed corolla and 5 long, curving stamens. The stamens and style extend beyond the corolla.

Bloom Season: May.

Habitat/Range: In thickets and along bogs and swamps. Found mainly in Connecticut, Rhode Island, Massachusetts, and Vermont. It is considered an endangered species in New Hampshire.

Comments: A very showy flowering shrub. The flowers often appear before or with the emerging leaves. As with most rhododendrons, all parts of the plant are toxic and should not be consumed by humans or animals.

CROWN VETCH
Coronilla varia
Bean Family (Fabaceae)

Description: A sprawling plant, typically 10–24" long, and nonhairy. The alternate leaves are compound and pinnately divided into 15–25 leaflets. Each leaflet is oblong and ½–1" long, with a smooth margin. The flowers are in dense, round clusters, long stalked, arising from the axils. Each flower has 5 pink and white petals.

Bloom Season: Late June–early August.

Habitat/Range: Fields, meadow, roadsides, and waste areas. Found throughout the region.

Comments: Introduced from Europe, it was mainly planted as a means to stabilize soil. The plant is toxic to horses and contains nitroglycosides. On a positive note, a number of bird and rodent species use Crown Vetch as ground cover.

TRAILING WILD BEAN
Strophostyles helvula
Bean Family (Fabaceae)

Description: A vine that can reach 6' in length and may be hairy. The leaves are divided into 3 leaflets, each ovate, often lobed, and ¾–3" long with a smooth margin. Several pale pink flowers are found in stalked clusters. Each flower is ¼–½" and displays the characteristic legume flower structure: a large upper petal, 2 lateral petals, and a fused lower petal.

Bloom Season: July–August.

Habitat/Range: Streamsides, thickets, and dry sandy soils. Found in Connecticut, Rhode Island, Massachusetts, and southeastern New Hampshire.

Comments: Native Americans rubbed leaves on skin affected by warts or by poison ivy.

RABBIT-FOOT CLOVER
Trifolium arvense
Bean Family (Fabaceae)

Description: An erect, freely branching plant, 4–16", with densely hairy stems and leaves. The compound leaves are alternate and divided into 3 leaflets, each of which is narrowly ovate or elliptical, hairy, and toothed at the tip. Flowers are pink to grayish pink in color and are in dense, egg-shaped or cylindrical-shaped heads. The heads are ¾–1½" long and have a fuzzy appearance.

Bloom Season: July–September.

Habitat/Range: Dry weedy areas, meadows, and roadsides. Common throughout the region.

Comments: Introduced from Europe, it is usually found growing in dense stands.

RED CLOVER
Trifolium pratense
Bean Family (Fabaceae)

Description: These plants can grow from 6–24" and are hairy or hairless. The leaves are divided into 3 leaflets. Each leaflet is ovate and ½–1" wide, with a smooth margin. A pale chevron can be seen on the leaf's upper surface. Flowers are in round, dense heads on erect stems. The pinkish red flower heads are up to 1½" wide. Each flower is composed of an upper showy petal (called a banner), 2 lateral petals (called wings), and 2 fused lower petals (called the keel).

Bloom Season: May–September.

Habitat/Range: Meadows, clearings, fields, roadsides, and lawns. Common throughout the region.

Comments: Originally from Europe, it was extensively planted in North America. A flower tea was used in folk medicine as an expectorant and mild sedative. It was also used to treat asthma, bronchitis, and coughs. The plant has been shown to contain a number of biologically active compounds and, in particular, high levels of phytoestrogens, a diverse group of plant compounds that have the ability to somewhat mimic the effects of human estrogen. Women, to help reduce the intensity of certain menopausal symptoms, sometimes use phytoestrogens. In addition, red clover is one of the few introduced species to be honored as a state flower—in this case, Vermont.

COMMON VETCH
Vicia sativa
Bean Family (Fabaceae)

Description: Climbing plant, 1–3' long, and hairy. The leaves are divided into 6–16 leaflets. Each leaflet is green, oblong to linear, up to 1½" long, and notched at the base, with a smooth margin. Stipules present are less than ¼". The pink flowers, 1–2, are found in the leaf axils and measure about ½–1".

Bloom Season: June–early August.

Habitat/Range: Fields, roadsides, and weedy areas. Commonly found throughout the region.

Comments: A cosmopolitan species that is found in every state except Utah.

HERB-ROBERT
Geranium robertianum
Geranium Family (Geraniaceae)

Description: This is a hairy-stemmed plant, 6–20" tall. The leaves are pinnately compound, divided into 3–5 lobes, and dark green in color. The flowers are found in pairs on the stalk, are pink to lavender, with 5 petals and up to ½" wide.

Bloom Season: Late May–August.

Habitat/Range: Damp woodlands, rocky woods, and ravines. Found throughout the region to southern Maine.

Comments: An introduced species from Europe. The leaves, when crushed, give off an unpleasant odor. Traditional folk medicine prescribed a leaf tea for treating a wide range of ailments from stomach and intestinal disorders to kidney infections, tuberculosis, and malaria.

BIFID HEMP-NETTLE
Galeopsis bifida
Mint Family (Lamiaceae)

Description: These plants are hairy and square stemmed and measure 6–30". The leaves are simple, opposite, ovate to elliptic, 1–4" long, stalked, and hairy, with a toothed margin. The flowers are found in whorls on terminal clusters. Each flower is pale pink with magenta markings on the lower petal. As with Hemp-Nettle, the calyx is 5 lobed and hairy, and the corolla is tube shaped. The lower petal is notched.

Bloom Season: July–August.

Habitat/Range: Fields, roadsides, and weedy areas. Found throughout the region.

Comments: Bifid Hemp-Nettle originated in Eurasia. It can be distinguished from Hemp-Nettle (*G. tetrahit*) by its notched lower petal.

PURPLE TRILLIUM
Trillium erectum
Bunch-Flower Family (Melanthiaceae)

Description: Plants range in height from 8–20". Leaves are in whorls of 3 at the base of the flower stalk. Each sessile leaf is diamond shaped, pointed at the tip, and displaying net veins. The dark green leaves have smooth margins. A single nodding flower, up to 3" in diameter, is borne on a 1–3" erect stalk. The 3 maroon petals are somewhat lanceolate and usually slightly recurving. Sepals, numbering 3, are green.

Bloom Season: Late April–May.

Habitat/Range: Moist rich woods. Found throughout the region.

Comments: A common name for this flower was Birthroot. This name derived from the fact that Native Americans and early colonists used the root in a powder form to help promote birth. Another more colorful common name was Stinking Benjamin. This name was aptly derived from the somewhat unpleasant-smelling flowers whose odor and color loosely mimics carrion as a means to attract flies, which are the plant's main pollinators.

VIRGINIA MEADOW BEAUTY

Rhexia virginica
Melastome Family (Melastomataceae)

Description: Plants are erect, 6–30", with a 4-sided, bristly, and slightly winged stem. The leaves are simple, opposite, narrowly ovate or ovate, and ¾–2" long, with a toothed margin and 3 prominent veins. The flowers are found on terminal racemes. Individual flowers are up to 1½" wide and pink with 4 petals and 8 prominent yellow stamens.

Bloom Season: July–early August.

Habitat/Range: Found in moist open areas throughout the region.

Comments: From the leaves and stems, Native Americans brewed a tea that they used as a throat cleanser.

FIREWEED

Chamerion angustifolium
Evening-Primrose Family (Onagraceae)

Description: Fireweed is an erect plant, growing 1–8' in height. The leaves are simple, alternate, lanceolate to linear, 1–8" in length, and sessile with a smooth margin. Numerous rose-pink flowers are found on terminal spikes. Each flower measures ¾–1" with 4 rounded and unequal petals, 8 stamens, and a downward-curving style that is hairy at its base.

Bloom Season: July–August.

Habitat/Range: Roadsides, clearings, and burned woodlands. Found throughout the region.

Comments: After an area has been cleared either by fire or other disturbance, this is one of the first arrivals to colonize the site.

GRASS-PINK ORCHID
Calopogon tuberosus
Orchid Family (Orchidaceae)

Description: The plant's wiry stem measures 4–24" tall. Each plant has a single basal leaf. The leaf is 4–10" long, linear, and green in color, with smooth margins. Three to 12 pink flowers are located on a terminal raceme. Individual flowers are 1–2" wide, with 5 oblong petals and sepals. The lip petal is ½–¾" in length and narrow, with yellow- or white-tipped hairs that are highly conspicuous. Usually only 1–3 flowers are in bloom at any given time.

Bloom Season: Mid-June–late July.

Habitat/Range: Acidic bogs, swamps, and damp meadows. These plants are found throughout the region.

Comments: Often found growing along with several other orchid species like Dragon's Mouth (*Arethusa bulbosa*) and Rose Pagonia (*Pagonia ophioglossoides*).

PINK LADY'S SLIPPER
Cypripedium acaule
Orchid Family (Orchidaceae)

Description: This common orchid stands 6–15" tall and is covered with fine hairs. The two basal leaves are simple, measuring 4–8" long, and elliptical in shape with a smooth margin. The upper leaf surface is dark green while the lower leaf surface is a pale silvery green. The flowers are solitary, terminal, and 2–4". The flower is composed of an inflated pouchlike lip petal that is pink with highly conspicuous, red, veinlike markings. A fissure or cleft runs down the front of the petal. There are 2 upper petals that are yellowish green to brown in color, lanceolate, 1–2" long, and twisted. Three yellowish green sepals are found above and below the lip petal.

Bloom Season: Late May–June.

Habitat/Range: Dry woodlands, acidic swamps, and pine woods. Found throughout the region.

Comments: The germinating seed requires interaction with a soil fungus to survive. The seedlings may be 4–5 years old before producing their first flower. The flower's color and fissure serve to attract bees as the primary pollinators. The bees enter the flower through the cleft in the front of the pouch petal. A less common white-flowered form (*C. acaule* forma *albiflorum*, pictured above) can be found scattered throughout the northern portion of the region. *C. acaule* is the official state wildflower of New Hampshire.

ROSE PAGONIA
Pogonia ophloglossoides
Orchid Family (Orchidaceae)

Description: A slender-stemmed orchid 6–20" tall. A single leaf is found about midway up the stem. The leaf is narrowly ovate and 1–3" long with a smooth margin. A solitary rose-pink flower sits atop the stem. There are 2 lateral petals and 1 lip petal and 3 sepals ranging in size from ½–1¾". The sepals are ovate while the lateral petals are elliptic. The somewhat spoon-shaped lip petal is bearded in the middle with yellow hairs.

Bloom Season: Mid-June–mid-July.

Habitat/Range: Wet meadows, bogs, and swamps. Found throughout the region.

Comments: This orchid frequently occurs in large colonies. Generally the plants have a solitary flower, but some individuals can have up to 2–3. An extremely rare white-flowered subspecies occurs in New England.

SMOOTH GERARDIA
Agalinis purpurea
Broom-Rape Family (Orobanchaceae)

Description: These spreading plants grow to 4–36" and are hairless. The leaves are simple, opposite, linear, ¾–1½" long, and ⅛" wide with a smooth margin. The flowers, few to many, are in the axils of the leaves. They are pink, purple, or occasionally white, short stalked, and ½–1", with 5 petals that have dark spots and are downy inside.

Bloom Season: Late July–early September.

Habitat/Range: Wet, acidic, and sandy soils. Found in Connecticut, Rhode Island, Massachusetts, southern New Hampshire, and southern Maine.

Comments: Gerardias are hemi-parasitic on the roots of other plants. Sand-Plain Gerardia (*A. acuta*) is limited to a few scattered locales in Connecticut, Rhode Island, and Massachusetts and is considered endangered.

TALL CORYDALIS
Corydalis sempervirens
Poppy Family (Papaveraceae)

Description: Tall Corydalis plants are 12–30" tall with bluish green foliage. The basal leaves are stalked, with 3–5 lobes and a smooth margin. The upper leaves are smaller and sessile. The flowers are on panicles. The flowers are ½" long and pink and yellow with 4 petals, creating a tube-shaped corolla with an upward-pointing spur.

Bloom Season: End of May–end of July.

Habitat/Range: Dry, rocky woodlands. Found throughout the region.

Comments: Native Americans used a plant decoction as a remedy for hemorrhoids.

LYON'S TURTLEHEAD
Chelone lyonii
Plantain Family (Plantaginaceae)

Description: Plants are erect and range in height from 1–3'. The leaves are simple, opposite, 4–7" long, narrowly ovate, rounded at the base, stalked (½–1"), and with a toothed margin. The tubular flowers range from pink to pinkish purple in color. The 2-lipped flowers are found on the stem in tight clusters in the axils of opposite leaves. The lower lip is bearded with tiny yellow hairs. Each flower measures 1–1¼". The flowers closely resemble White Turtlehead.

Bloom Season: Mid-July–end of August.

Habitat/Range: Similar habitat to White Turtlehead. In New England this is an uncommon species. Reported in Connecticut, Rhode Island, and Maine. When encountered in the wild, it is probably a garden escape.

Comments: The common name honors the 19th-century American botanist John Lyons.

FRINGED POLYGALA
Polygala paucifolia
Milkwort Family (Polygalaceae)

Description: Small plants, 3–6" tall. The scalelike lower leaves are less than ¼" long. The upper leaves are simple, alternate, elliptic to ovate, and ½–4" long with a smooth margin. The flowers are violet-pink (rarely white) and ½–1" long. They arise from a long stalk from the axils of the upper leaves. Each plant typically has 1–4 flowers. The flower has 3 petals that form a tubular structure. The lower petal lip is fringed at the tip. There are 5 sepals, with the lateral 2 forming the "wings" of the flower.

Bloom Season: May–June.

Habitat/Range: Moist, rich woodlands throughout the region.

Comments: This tiny plant with its orchidlike flower is a real spring beauty.

FIELD MILKWORT
Polygala sanguinea
Milkwort Family (Polygalaceae)

Description: Plants range from 3–15". The leaves are simple, linear, and up to 1½" long, with a smooth margin. The rose-pink flowers are on dense, cylindrical racemes up to 1½" long. Individual flowers are ⅛" and have 3 petals and 5 sepals. The inner 2 sepals form a wing.

Bloom Season: July–early October.

Habitat/Range: Open woodlands, meadows, and fields. Found throughout the region.

Comments: Although this plant will do well in loamy soils, its preference is for soils that are sandy and rocky.

LONG-BRISTLED SMARTWEED
Polygonum caespitosum
Smartweed Family (Polygonaceae)

Description: Sprawling plants to 3' long and somewhat branched. The leaves range from 1–3" and are lanceolate and short stalked (¼" or less), with a smooth margin. There are sheaths around the leaf nodes that are characteristically long (up to ½") and bristly. The flowers are borne on narrow erect spikes. Each flower is ⅛" or less and pink in color. Petals are absent.

Bloom Season: July–early October.

Habitat/Range: Found along ponds and various types of waste areas. Occurs throughout Connecticut, Rhode Island, Massachusetts, and Vermont to southern New Hampshire.

Comments: Originally from eastern Asia, it is readily distinguished from other smartweeds by the long bristles on the leaf sheaths.

LADY'S THUMBS

Polygonum persicaria
Smartweed Family (Polygonaceae)

Description: A sprawling, reddish-stemmed plant, growing up to 2'. The leaves are narrowly ovate, 3–6" long, and stalked (¼–½"), with a short fringe on the leaf sheath, a smooth margin, and a purplish blotch in the middle of each leaf. The flowers are found on one to several spikes. Each spike is about ½–2" tall and densely covered with flowers. Each flower is pink to pale purple, no more than ⅛" with 4–6 sepals. Petals are absent.

Bloom Season: July–early October.

Habitat/Range: Common throughout the region and usually found in weedy areas.

Comments: Introduced from Europe. A leaf tea was used in European folk medicine to aid in easing inflammation, sore throats, and stomachaches. Native Americans used the plant in a similar manner but also included it for treating poison-ivy rash.

SHEEP SORREL

Rumex acetosella
Smartweed Family (Polygonaceae)

Description: The plants range from 4–12" tall. The leaves are 1–2" long and have a characteristic arrowhead shape. The leaf margins are smooth, and the basal lobes curve outward. The nodding flowers are borne on spikelike clusters. The flowers are initially green in color and then turn red. Individual flowers measure a mere ¹⁄₁₆". Male and female flowers reside on separate plants.

Bloom Season: May–July.

Habitat/Range: Found in open areas with poor acidic-type soils. Widespread throughout the region.

Comments: A European introduction, Sheep Sorrel has naturalized throughout New England and serves as a major source of food for many bird species. The plant favors acidic soils low in nutrients and often forms pure stands in this type of habitat. A leaf tea was used in European folk medicine to treat fevers and inflammation. Roots were prepared in a tea for controlling diarrhea and menstrual bleeding. The plants are rich in vitamin C and carotenoids. The leaves have a pungent and sour taste due to the presence of high concentrations of potassium oxalate crystals.

WILD COLUMBINE
Aquilegia canadensis
Crowfoot Family (Ranunculaceae)

Description: This is a branching plant 6–30" in height. The basal leaves are stalked, compound, each divided into 3-lobed leaflets. The stem leaves are greatly reduced. The solitary flowers are red and yellow, nodding, bell-shaped, and 1–2" long. There are 5 red sepals and 5 yellow petals, each having a backward-pointing spurlike projection that contains the nectar. Yellow stamens are clustered together and protrude beyond the petals.

Bloom Season: Mid-May–June.

Habitat/Range: Dry woodlands, rocky ledges, and open slopes. Found throughout the region except for northern Maine.

Comments: Mainly pollinated by hummingbirds and long-tongued insects. Native Americans used a tiny amount of seeds to treat and reduce fevers and headaches. Seeds were also rubbed into the hair to help control lice. The plant's roots were used to treat diarrhea and stomachaches and as a diuretic.

QUEEN-OF-THE-PRAIRIE
Filipendula rubra
Rose Family (Rosaceae)

Description: Plants are erect, 2–5' tall, and hairless. The compound leaves are pinnately divided into 5–9 leaflets, each up to 4" long, and either lobed or toothed. Numerous pink to red flowers are found on a showy terminal panicle. Each flower measures ¼–½", with 5 petals, 5 sepals, and numerous protruding stamens that give the cluster a feathery appearance.

Bloom Season: July–mid-August.

Habitat/Range: Found in low woodlands, wet meadows, and thickets throughout the region.

Comments: The high tannin content of the roots made it a popular folk medicine for treating diarrhea and dysentery.

BEACH ROSE
Rosa rugosa
Rose Family (Rosaceae)

Description: A branching plant, 2–6' high, with hairy twigs and prickly stems. The leaves are alternate and pinnately compound and divided into 7–9 leaflets. Each leaflet is 1–2" long, oblong, and dark green, and with a toothed margin. The upper leaf surface is wrinkled, and the lower surface is smooth. The pink-lavender (sometimes white) flowers are solitary, arising in the leaf axils. The flowers are 2–4" wide, with 5 rounded petals, 5 reflexed sepals, a yellow center, and numerous pistils and stamens.

Bloom Season: Early July–mid-August.

Habitat/Range: Thickets, roadsides, and beaches. Scattered throughout the region.

Comments: Originally from Asia. A garden escape, it can now be found naturalized in scattered locales throughout New England. The fruit of Beach Rose is high in vitamin C and was used to treat scurvy. The Chinese used both the fruit and flowers to treat ailments such as rheumatism, stomachaches, and dysentery, to name a few.

VIRGINIA ROSE
Rosa virginiana
Rose Family (Rosaceae)

Description: A small bushy shrub, 1–6' tall, with hairy stems. The leaves are divided into 5–9 dark green leaflets, ovate in shape, 1–2½" long, with a toothed margin and smooth and shiny surface. The few to many pink flowers are 2–3" wide with 5 petals, 5 sepals, and numerous stamens.

Bloom Season: July–early August.

Habitat/Range: Fields, thickets, clearings, and shorelines. Found throughout the region.

Comments: Native Americans used the bark and roots for a variety of medicinal purposes. The rose hips (the fruit), as in most rose species, is a rich source of vitamin C and can be eaten.

PURPLE FLOWERING RASPBERRY
Rubus odoratus
Rose Family (Rosaceae)

Description: Plants are 3–6' tall, branching, and lacking prickles. The leaves are simple, 3–8" long, and alternate and look like maple leaves, with 3–5 pointed lobes and a heart-shaped base. The flowers are in loose axial clusters. The flowers are deep pink and 1–2" wide, with 5 rounded petals and numerous stamens and pistils.

Bloom Season: June–July.

Habitat/Range: Woodland edges, thickets, roadsides, and moist, shady areas. Found throughout the region.

Comments: Although the fruit contains an abundance of seeds, it is quite tasty. Native Americans often dried the fruit for subsequent consumption during the lean winter months.

133

HARDHACK
Spiraea tomentosa
Rose Family (Rosaceae)

Description: An erect, shrubby plant up to 4' tall, with woolly stems. The leaves are simple, alternate, oblong, 1–2" long, with a toothed margin. The upper leaf surface is green, and the lower surface is more whitish and hairy. The rose-pink flowers are on dense terminal panicles that are 3–5" tall. Individual flowers are no more than ⅛" wide, with 5 petals and 5 sepals.

Bloom Season: July–mid-August.

Habitat/Range: Wet meadows, swamps, and old fields. Common throughout the range.

Comments: Native Americans made a leaf tea to treat diarrhea and dysentery and a flower tea to combat morning sickness.

YELLOW AND ORANGE FLOWERS

Flowers in this section range from creamy pale yellow to bright glossy yellow to orange. Some pale yellow forms may grade to a pale green hue. The green and white sections should also be checked in this book.

WILD PARSNIP
Pastinaca sativa
Umbel Family (Apiaceae)

Description: Plants are generally 2–5' tall and have a grooved stem. The leaves are alternate, pinnately compound, and divided into 5–15 leaflets. Each leaflet is oblong to ovate and 2–4" long, with a toothed margin. Numerous tiny flowers are on umbels. Each umbel has 15–25 spokes and is 2–6" wide. The yellow flowers are roughly ⅛" wide and have 5 petals.

Bloom Season: June–July.

Habitat/Range: Found in fields, roadsides, and various types of waste areas throughout the region.

Comments: This species is a European introduction.

GOLDEN ALEXANDERS

Zizia aurea
Umbel Family (Apiaceae)

Description: These smooth plants generally top off at 3'. The compound leaves are twice divided, creating up to 9 leaflets. The leaflets are ovate and 1–2" long with a toothed margin. Flowers are in a flat-topped umbel. The umbel measures 1–2" in width and has 6–20 spokes. The individual flowers are small, ⅛", and yellow in color, with 5 petals.

Bloom Season: Mid-May–June.

Habitat/Range: Wet woodlands, moist fields, and shorelines. Found throughout the region.

Comments: A root tea preparation was used to treat syphilis and to reduce fevers. Caution: Plant is toxic.

ORANGE MILKWEED

Asclepias tuberosa
Dogbane Family (Apocynaceae)

Description: Plants are 1–3' tall, hairy, and quite leafy. This plant has a nonmilky sap, unusual for a milkweed species. The leaves are alternate (as opposed to opposite, as found in most milkweed species) and lanceolate and measure 1–5" long. The leaves have a pointed tip and smooth margins and are dark green. Numerous flowers are on rounded terminal clusters. Flowers are yellow to bright orange in color. Individual flowers measure ¼–⅜" wide with 5 highly recurved petals creating a crownlike effect around the central disk.

Bloom Season: Late June–August.

Habitat/Range: Dry woodlands, fields, and roadsides. Found throughout Connecticut, Massachusetts, and Rhode Island. This species is uncommon or absent in the northern parts of the region.

Comments: Also called Butterfly Milkweed or Pleurisy Root. Used by Native Americans and early physicians to treat pleurisy and other lung infections. This species also has a long fibrous taproot that aids in drought resistance. Like all milkweeds, it contains numerous cardiac glycosides.

BUR-MARIGOLD
Bidens cernua
Composite Family (Asteraceae)

Description: Plants are 1–3' tall with leaves that are simple, opposite, narrowly ovate to lanceolate, 1–8" long, and sessile, with a toothed margin. The numerous yellow heads are found in the upper leaf axils. Each flower head is nodding, ½–1½" wide, with 6–8 rays. The rays have a short length in relation to the width of the disk. There are numerous disk flowers, each tubular with 5 lobes and measuring less than ⅛".

Bloom Season: Mid-August–September.

Habitat/Range: Swamps, stream banks, and other wet and muddy areas. Found throughout the region.

Comments: The seeds of *Bidens* species readily adhere to fur and clothing, thereby greatly facilitating their dispersal.

PURPLE-STEM BEGGERTICK
Bidens connata
Composite Family (Asteraceae)

Description: Plants are 6–36", hairless, and with green or purple stems. The leaves measure 1–8" long, are elliptic to ovate in shape and stalked, with a toothed margin. The flower heads are yellow and up to ¾" wide. Rays are usually absent, but when present are inconspicuous, measuring less than ¼" in length.

Bloom Season: July–late September.

Habitat/Range: Wet places and weedy areas. Found throughout the region.

Comments: European physicians used extracts to induce urination, menstruation, and sweating. Native Americans brewed a tea for use in expelling worms. They also chewed the leaves to help alleviate a sore throat.

LANCE-LEAVED COREOPSIS
Coreopsis lanceolata
Composite Family (Asteraceae)

Description: Erect plants, 6–30", hairless or slightly hairy. The leaves are simple and opposite. The basal leaves and lower stem leaves are stalked in contrast to the upper stem leaves that are sessile. The leaves are 2–8" long and narrowly ovate to linear. The flower heads, 1 to several, are bright yellow and daisylike. Each head is 1½–2½" wide and long stalked, and composed of numerous disk flowers and 6–10 rays. At the tip of each ray there are 3–5 notches.

Bloom Season: Late May–July.

Habitat/Range: Found in fields, roadsides, and sandy soils throughout the region.

Comments: *C. lanceolata* often forms extensive colonies in its favored habitats.

SLENDER FRAGRANT GOLDENROD
Euthamia tenuifolia
Composite Family (Asteraceae)

Description: Plants range from 1–3' tall, with a hairless to finely hairy stem that branches above midstem. The leaves are simple, linear, pointed at the tip, and 1–5" long, with a single prominent vein and a smooth margin. Tiny resinous dots are also found on the leaves. Numerous yellow flower heads are in flat-topped clusters located on each branch. Each ¼" head has 6–16 rays.

Bloom Season: August–late September.

Habitat/Range: Open areas. Found in Connecticut, Rhode Island, Massachusetts, western Vermont, and eastern New Hampshire.

Comments: Common Flat-Topped Goldenrod (*E. graminifolia*), a similar-appearing species in the region, has lanceolate leaves with 3–5 prominent veins.

139

PURPLE-HEADED SNEEZEWEED
Helenium flexuosum
Composite Family (Asteraceae)

Description: Plants have a winged stem and are 6–36" tall. The leaves are simple, alternate, narrowly ovate to linear, 1–4" long, and sessile. The flower heads are found in flat-topped clusters and are daisylike. Each flower is about 1" wide, with a reddish brown to purple central disk surrounded by 8–13 yellow petal-like rays that are 3-lobed at the tips.

Bloom Season: July–August.

Habitat/Range: Fields, meadows, and disturbed areas. Found throughout the region to southern Maine.

Comments: Native Americans used the leaves in powdered form to induce sneezing. Sensitive individuals may develop dermatitis when handling the plant.

THIN-LEAVED SUNFLOWER
Helianthus decapetalus
Composite Family (Asteraceae)

Description: This sunflower grows to a height of 5' and is hairless. The leaves are 3–10" long and elliptic to ovate, with stalks that are ½–3" long and a toothed margin. The flower heads are 1–4" wide with a yellow central disk and 8–16 yellow rays. The involucral bracts are elliptic and somewhat loosely formed.

Bloom Season: Late July–September.

Habitat/Range: Found in woodlands and thickets throughout the region.

Comments: This attractive sunflower can form large vegetative colonies from rhizomes.

WOODLAND SUNFLOWER
Helianthus strumosus
Composite Family (Asteraceae)

Description: Plants range from 3–8' in height and are hairless or with a slightly rough-textured stem. The leaves are elliptic to ovate, 3–7" long, and stalked, with a somewhat toothed or toothless margin and a rough-textured upper surface and a smooth lower surface. The flower heads, several to many, are terminal and 2–4" wide, with a yellow central disk surrounded by 8–15 bright yellow rays. The involucral bracts are somewhat elliptic and loose.

Bloom Season: Mid-July–late September.

Habitat/Range: Thickets and woodland openings and borders. Found throughout the region to central Maine.

Comments: Native Americans used root preparations as a worm expellant.

ORANGE HAWKWEED
Hieracium aurantiacum
Composite Family (Asteraceae)

Description: Plants can reach a height of up to 24". The leaves are basal and form a rosette. Leaves are oblong, 2–8" long, and hairy on both surfaces, with a smooth margin. Five to 30 orange flower heads are found on a flat-topped panicle. The end of each ray is notched with 5 teeth. The green bracts are covered with black, gland-tipped hairs.

Bloom Season: June–August.

Habitat/Range: Meadows, fields, and roadsides. Common throughout the region.

Comments: Although native to Europe, this plant has naturalized in the region. This species can reproduce rapidly either by seed or by stolons. It is often encountered growing in large and often dense colonies, which, when in flower, can be a beautiful sight.

YELLOW KING-DEVIL

Hieracium caespitosum
Composite Family (Asteraceae)

Description: This introduced species grows 6–36" in height with a hairy stem and white sap. The leaves form as a basal rosette. Individual leaves are oblong, broader at the tip, hairy both on the upper and lower surfaces, and measuring 2–10" in length, with a smooth margin. The flower stalk is usually leafless although an occasional leaf or two may appear on the stalk. The bright yellow flowers, 5–30, are borne on a compact cluster on top of a tall hairy stalk. The flowers appear dandelion-like, and the rays have a squared off and toothed edge.

Bloom Season: May–August.

Habitat/Range: Roadsides, fields, grasslands, and pastures. Common throughout the region.

Comments: This plant was originally introduced from Europe. It is often found growing in dense colonies. The adult plants have a tendency to produce numerous daughter plants from above-ground runners called stolons. European folk medicine used preparations of the plant to treat a variety of lung ailments.

VIRGINIA DWARF DANDELION

Krigia virginica
Composite Family (Asteraceae)

Description: Plants grow 1–12" tall. Early leaves are round, with smooth margins. As the plant grows, later leaves appear that are lanceolate to narrowly ovate, lobed, measuring 1–4" long. The flower heads are solitary and appear on long stalks. Yellow petal-like rays surround a yellow center. Involucral bracts are reflexed.

Bloom Season: May–early July.

Habitat/Range: Sandy, dry places and rocky outcrops. Found in Connecticut, Rhode Island, and Massachusetts to central Vermont and central New Hampshire. May be extirpated in Maine.

Comments: *K. virginica* bears a superficial resemblance to the Common Dandelion (*T. officinale*) but with smaller flower heads and lighter green foliage.

WILD LETTUCE
Lactuca canadensis
Composite Family (Asteraceae)

Description: These are large, erect plants that can grow up to 10' tall. Plants are usually hairless and contain a milky sap. The highly variable leaves are simple, alternate, narrowly ovate, toothless, toothed, or highly lobed, 4–12" long, and sessile without prickles on either leaf surface. Numerous pale yellow flower heads are found on panicles. The heads are dandelion-like, each about ¼" wide.

Bloom Season: Late June–August.

Habitat/Range: Woodland edges, fields, and disturbed areas. Common throughout the region.

Comments: Native Americans and the early colonists used the milky sap to treat various skin problems and used a plant tea as a sedative and pain reliever.

HEART-LEAVED GROUNDSEL
Packera aurea
Composite Family (Asteraceae)

Description: Also known as Golden Ragwort, this plant ranges from 10–36" tall and has daisylike flowers. The plant is hairy when young but becomes hairless with age. Basal leaves are heart shaped, up to 4" long, and stalked with toothed margins. The stem leaves are smaller lanceolate and clasping, with lobes. Flower heads are golden-yellow in color and found in terminal clusters. Individual flower heads measure ½–¾" wide, with 8–12 yellow petal-like rays surrounding a yellow center.

Bloom Season: Late May–June.

Habitat/Range: Moist woodlands, wet meadows, and swampy areas. Common throughout the region.

Comments: Native Americans prepared teas from both the roots and the leaves to treat menstrual problems as well as complications associated with childbirth. This usage led to the plant commonly being referred to as Squaw Root. The plant was also used to treat dysentery and lung ailments.

RUNNING GROUNDSEL
Packera obovata
Composite Family (Asteraceae)

Description: Plants are erect and 6–30" tall, with daisylike flowers. Like Heart-Leaved Groundsel, the plant starts off hairy then becomes hairless with age. The basal leaves are ovate to round and 1–8" long, with a toothed margin. The smaller stem leaves are lanceolate, lobed, and clasping. The flower heads are on flat-topped panicles. Each flower head measures ½–1½" wide, with the disk ¼–½" wide. Golden-yellow, petal-like rays surround a yellow disk.

Bloom Season: May–June.

Habitat/Range: Rich woodlands and rocky outcrops. Found in Connecticut and Massachusetts to southern New Hampshire and Vermont.

Comments: Once established, this species spreads rapidly.

BLACK-EYED SUSAN
Rudbeckia hirta
Composite Family (Asteraceae)

Description: At 1–3' tall this plant has a rough, hairy, and minutely grooved stem. The leaves are simple, alternate, elliptic to ovate, 2–5" long, and hairy with a smooth or toothed margin. The lower leaves are stalked while the upper stem leaves are sessile. The flower heads are solitary, daisylike, 2–4" wide, with a cone-shaped brown disk and surrounded by 8–20 yellow rays. The involucral bracts are narrowly ovate to linear in shape and very hairy.

Bloom Season: July–August.

Habitat/Range: Woodland edges, fields, meadows, and roadsides throughout the region.

Comments: Native Americans brewed a root tea to treat colds and to expel worms. It was also used as a wash for surface sores and snakebites. Earaches were treated with the juice obtained from the roots. Some individuals may develop a contact dermatitis from simply handling the plant.

BLUE-STEMMED GOLDENROD
Solidago caesia
Composite Family (Asteraceae)

Description: Plants grow 1–3' tall, with stems frequently tinged blue or purple. The leaves are simple, alternate, narrowly ovate, 1–7" long, sharply pointed at the tip, and hairless or nearly so, with a toothed margin. The flower heads are in short axillary clusters. Individual flower heads are about ¼" wide with 3–8 yellow petal-like rays.

Bloom Season: Mid-August–October.

Habitat/Range: Found in woodlands and thickets throughout the region.

Comments: *S. caesia* is one of the few species of goldenrod found to grow in shaded places.

TALL GOLDENROD
Solidago canadensis var. *scabra*
Composite Family (Asteraceae)

Description: Erect plants 2–7' tall and usually nonbranching. The leaves are simple, lanceolate, with a somewhat rough texture, and sessile, with a smooth or moderately toothed margin. The lower leaves are up to 6" long. Leaves continue to reduce in size with increasing stem height. The flowers are found on terminal branches that form a cluster with a pyramid-like shape. Individual flowers are ⅛" and yellow in color.

Bloom Season: Mid-July–early October.

Habitat/Range: Fields, thickets, and roadsides. Commonly found throughout the region.

Comments: Tall Goldenrod used to be classified as a separate species, *S. altissima.* It is now considered a variant of *S. canadensis.* Native Americans made a tea from the flowers to treat fevers and snakebites. Sore throats were reduced in severity by chewing the crushed flowers. Leaf extracts have been shown to be diuretic.

HAIRY GOLDENROD
Solidago hispida
Composite Family (Asteraceae)

Description: Erect, usually nonbranching, plants that can reach 3' in height. Both the stem and leaves are hairy. The leaves are simple, alternate, 1–6" long, and usually sessile, with a smooth margin. Flower heads are clustered near and on top of the stem. The heads are about ¼" wide with 6–16 yellow rays.

Bloom Season: Late July–early October.

Habitat/Range: Dry open areas with sandy or rocky soil. Found throughout the region.

Comments: Similar to Silverrod.

ROUGH-STEMMED GOLDENROD
Solidago rugosa
Composite Family (Asteraceae)

Description: Plants are 1–6' tall and very hairy stemmed. The leaves are narrowly ovate or elliptic, 1–5" long, rough textured, and slightly hairy on the ribs below, with a toothed margin. The flower heads are clustered mostly on the upper side of arching branches that form a triangular panicle. Each head is ⅛–¼" wide and surrounded with 6–11 yellow rays.

Bloom Season: July–early September.

Habitat/Range: Fields, thickets, open areas, and roadsides. Found throughout the region.

Comments: A highly variable species but one that can be readily distinguished from other goldenrod species by its rather hairy stem.

COMMON TANSY
Tanacetum vulgare
Composite Family (Asteraceae)

Description: These plants are 2–4' tall, with a somewhat woody stem. The leaves are alternate, deeply lobed, and twice divided into linear segments, resulting in a fernlike appearance. The leaves measure 3–7" in length and have toothed margins. Leaves have numerous small glands and, when crushed, emit a highly aromatic odor. The flowers are numerous and found on flat-topped panicles. Each orange-yellow flower is ¼–½" wide with a button-shaped disk. Ray flowers are generally absent but may be present on occasion.

Bloom Season: July–early September.

Habitat/Range: Fields, roadsides, and weedy areas. Found scattered throughout the region.

Comments: Common Tansy was originally introduced from Europe. A diluted leaf tea was once used in folk medicine to treat conditions such as jaundice, sore throats, worms, and dyspepsia as well as to suppress menses. Leaves have been shown to have insecticidal properties. Caution: The leaves' highly aromatic oils may cause dermatitis in sensitive individuals. If enough of the oil is ingested, it can be lethal.

COMMON DANDELION
Taraxacum officinale
Composite Family (Asteraceae)

Description: Common Dandelion grows 2–18" tall from a thick taproot and has a hollow stem and milky sap. The leaves are simple, basal, narrowly ovate, deeply lobed, 2–8" long, and sessile, with a coarsely toothed margin. The flower heads are solitary and sit atop a long, slender stalk. Heads measure ¾–1½" wide with numerous (100–300) yellow rays. There are no disk flowers. Each ray has 5 tiny teeth marking the edge. There are 2 rows of bracts, with the outer row being reflexed. The flowers only open during the daytime and are even closed during overcast days. Each flower head can strongly reflect ultraviolet light, a feature that may serve as nectar guides for many insect species.

Bloom Season: April–September (and even in the winter in some parts of New England if the temperatures are mild enough).

Habitat/Range: Fields, weedy places, meadows, roadsides, and lawns.

Comments: Originally a native plant of Eurasia, it made its way to North America from Europe, being brought over by the early settlers. The name dandelion is derived from the old French *dent-de-lion,* or tooth of the lion, a reference to the shape of the leaves. Dandelion is a cosmopolitan plant and the scourge of many a modern-day home owner. The highly recognizable ball-shaped, grayish white seed heads contain numerous parachute seeds that are readily dispersed. A hooklike hair is located at the end of each seed. This structure facilitates the seed's attachment to a passing animal or to the soil upon landing. The leaves and flowers are rich in vitamins A and C and a variety of minerals. The leaves are often eaten in salads or can be cooked and eaten like spinach. A tea made from the roots was used as a diuretic and to treat kidney and bladder ailments. The roots were eaten like potatoes and were also ground and roasted for use as a coffeelike drink or as a coffee additive. The flower stems are the only part of the plant that cannot be eaten.

SHOWY GOAT'S BEARD
Tragopogon pratensis
Composite Family (Asteraceae)

Description: An erect plant, 6–30" tall, with a milky sap. The leaves are grasslike, long pointed, and up to 12" in length and clasping. The yellow flower heads are solitary and long stalked (1–3"). The flower head is composed entirely of ray flowers. The involucral bracts are about equal in length to the rays. The flowers open in the early morning and are usually closed by noon. The plants produce fluffy seed balls that are similar in appearance to those produced by dandelions, only much larger.

Bloom Season: May–July.

Habitat/Range: Fields, roadsides, and waste areas. Found throughout the region.

Comments: Yellow Goat's Beard (*T. dubius*), also from Europe, can be differentiated from *T. pratensis* by pointed bracts that are longer than the rays and by the swollen stem beneath the flower heads.

COLTSFOOT
Tussilago farfara
Composite Family (Asteraceae)

Description: The leaves of Coltsfoot do not emerge until after flowering has ended and continue to grow through the season. The 2–8" long basal leaves are simple, round to heart shaped, and white-woolly underneath, with a slightly toothed margin. A solitary yellow flower head, approximately 1" in diameter, sits atop a scaly stalk. The disk flowers are surrounded by numerous thin yellow rays and have a dandelion-like appearance.

Bloom Season: Mid-March–early May.

Habitat/Range: Disturbed areas, roadsides, and meadows. Found throughout New England.

Comments: This monotypic species was introduced from Europe. European folk medicine made teas from the leaves and flowers that were used in treating a variety of respiratory illnesses.

JEWELWEED
Impatiens capensis
Touch-Me-Not Family (Balsaminaceae)

Description: Jewelweed plants range from 2–5' tall and are branched with a smooth, nearly clear, succulent stem. The pale green leaves are simple, alternate, and long stemmed, with a smooth margin. The flowers are solitary, yellowish orange with numerous reddish brown blotches, and measure about 1" long. They are nodding, horn-shaped with a downward-curved spur that measures ¼–½" long.

Bloom Season: July–early September.

Habitat/Range: Shaded, moist woodlands, wet meadows, and along brooks and streams. Commonly found throughout the region.

Comments: Sap from the stem and leaves has been used to relieve the intensity and duration of the itch from poison ivy. In addition, the plant has been used to treat athlete's foot. Hummingbirds are a chief pollinator of Jewelweed.

JAPANESE BARBERRY
Berberis thunbergii
Barberry Family (Berberiaceae)

Description: A many-branched plant measuring 2–5' tall. Leaves are dark green to purple and ovate with a smooth margin. A single spine emerges from the junction of a leaf stem and branch. The pale yellow flowers are found solitary or in groups of 2–4, along the branches in the leaf axils. Individual flowers are globe shaped with 6 petals.

Bloom Season: Mid-May–mid-June.

Habitat/Range: Woodlands, pastures, and thickets. Found throughout the region.

Comments: This introduced species can grow from seed and from root creepers and often forms dense thickets that can quickly reduce plant diversity and alter the surrounding soil chemistry. This plant is considered a serious invasive species in Connecticut and Massachusetts. Several other barberry species readily grow in the region. Common Barberry can be distinguished from Japanese Barberry by its branched spines and long flower clusters containing as many as 30 individual flowers. American Barberry, a less common native species, has flower petals that are notched.

COMMON WINTERCRESS
Barbarea vulgaris
Mustard Family (Brassicaceae)

Description: This smooth-stemmed plant ranges from 6–30". The basal leaves are stalked and ovate, with 2–8 lobes and a smooth margin. The stem leaves are reduced and clasping. The flowers are found, several to many, in elongated clusters. Each flower is bright yellow and ¼–⅜" wide, with 4 ovate petals that form a cross shape.

Bloom Season: Mid-May–mid-June.

Habitat/Range: Meadows, roadsides, and moist fields. Common throughout the region.

Comments: Common Wintercress was originally introduced from Eurasia. Native Americans made a leaf tea to treat coughs and to use as a diuretic and an appetite stimulant. The young leaves and flowers have often been eaten in salads. However, recent clinical research has suggested a link between ingesting the plant and potential kidney damage.

FROSTWEED
Helianthemum canadense
Rock-Rose Family (Cistaceae)

Description: An erect, branching plant 6–24". The dull green leaves are ovate, densely hairy underneath, and 1–1½" long, with a smooth margin. Flowers are solitary and found on top of the stem. Each flower has 5 yellow petals and numerous stamens, measures ½–1½" in width, and has a hairy calyx. Flowers only open in full sunlight and persist for 1 day. Later in the growing season inconspicuous flowers lacking petals arise in the leaf axils. Each flower is approximately ⅛" with 3–4 stamens.

Bloom Season: May–June.

Habitat/Range: Rocky woodlands, clearings, and dry, sandy areas. Found throughout the region to northern Vermont, New Hampshire, and Maine.

Comments: Native Americans treated kidney ailments with a leaf tea. Early physicians once used a strong leaf-tea mixture to treat diarrhea, dysentery, and syphilis.

SESSILE BELLWORT
Uvularia sessifolia
Colchicum Family (Colchicaceae)

Description: A smooth plant, 4–12" tall, with an angled stem. The leaves are 1–3" long, narrowly ovate, and sessile. The upper leaf surface is light green and whitish green on the underside, and the margin is smooth. One to several pale yellow flowers are found atop the stem. The flowers are nodding, somewhat bell shaped, and up to 1" long with 2 petals and 3 petal-like sepals.

Bloom Season: April–June.

Habitat/Range: Woodlands and thickets. Found throughout the region.

Comments: Native Americans used a root tea to treat diarrhea. A root tea was used in folk medicine as a gargle for sore throats.

BUSH HONEYSUCKLE
Diervilla lonicera
Bush-Honeysuckle Family (Diervllaceae)

Description: A small (1–4' tall) shrub. The leaves are simple, opposite, ovate to narrowly ovate, 3–6" long, and stalked with a pointed tip and a minutely toothed margin. One to 5 flowers are found on terminal racemes. Each flower is pale yellow, ½–¾" long, tubular with 5 petal-like lobes that are recurved.

Bloom Season: June–July.

Habitat/Range: Woodlands and dry rocky soils. Found throughout the region.

Comments: Once pollinated, the flower noticeably changes color from pale yellow to a rich yellow-orange.

WILD INDIGO

Baptisia tinctoria
Bean Family (Fabaceae)

Description: A bushy plant, 1–3' tall, with grayish blue foliage. The compound leaves are divided into 3 leaflets. Each leaflet is ovate and ¾–1½" long, with a smooth margin. The flowers are on terminal racemes that are 2–4" tall. Each flower is yellow, pea-like, and up to ½".

Bloom Season: Late May–August.

Habitat/Range: Dry, sandy soils especially in fields. Found in Connecticut, Rhode Island, and Massachusetts to southern Vermont and New Hampshire. Considered endangered in Maine.

Comments: Historically used as a medicinal herb for the treatment of a variety of ailments.

WILD SENSITIVE PLANT

Chamaecrista nictitans
Bean Family (Fabaceae)

Description: Plants erect to arching, 6–15", and thin stemmed. The leaves are alternate, pinnately compound, with 12–30 leaflets. Each leaflet is oblong, ¼–½" long and pointed, with a smooth margin. They are somewhat sensitive to the touch, often responding by folding. The 1–3 yellow flowers are found in axillary clusters. Each flower measures about ¼" and has unequal-sized petals and 5 stamens.

Bloom Season: Late July–early September.

Habitat/Range: Dry woodlands and weedy areas with dry sandy soils. Found in Connecticut, Rhode Island, and Massachusetts to the extreme southern tip of Vermont. Considered endangered in New Hampshire.

Comments: Native Americans used a root tea preparation to combat fatigue.

BIRD'S-FOOT TREFOIL
Lotus corniculatus
Bean Family (Fabaceae)

Description: A trailing or erect, highly branched plant, 6–24", with cloverlike leaves. The compound leaves are divided into 3 leaflets, each of which is elliptic to ovate and up to ½" long, with a smooth margin. At the base of the stalk are 2 small, leaflike stipules. Found on flat terminal clusters are 2–8 flowers. Each flower is bright yellow to orange in color, pea-like, and up to ½". The plant requires 16 hours of daylight in order to produce flowers. The pod arrangement somewhat resembles a bird's foot. As the flower matures, it becomes tinged with red.

Bloom Season: Mid-June–August.

Habitat/Range: Meadows, fields, roadsides, and moist areas. Found throughout the region.

Comments: This plant, originally from Europe, can form dense mats that ultimately shade out other species. It has an extensive root system containing root nodules with the ability to fix nitrogen.

YELLOW SWEET CLOVER
Melilotus officinalis
Bean Family (Fabaceae)

Description: Yellow Sweet Clover grows as an erect or ascending plant, 2–7', and is loosely branching and hairless. The compound leaves are divided into 3 leaflets each of which is narrowly ovate, broadest at the tip, and up to 1" long, with a smooth margin. The flowers are on tall (2–5") racemes, originating in the leaf axils. Each yellow pea flower is about ¼" long.

Bloom Season: July–late September.

Habitat/Range: Commonly found along roadsides and in fields and weedy areas throughout the region.

Comments: Introduced from Eurasia. Folk medicine used a leaf tea to treat varicose veins. A tea made from the dried flowering plant treated ailments ranging from rheumatism to painful menstruation.

HOP-CLOVER
Trifolium aureum
Bean Family (Fabaceae)

Description: These highly branched, erect plants grow 6–16" tall. The leaves are on short stalks measuring ¼–½" long and are divided into 3 leaflets. Each leaflet is narrowly ovate or ovate, broader towards the tip, and notched. Numerous tiny (¼") yellow pea flowers are in an oblong cluster that is stalked and measures ½–1" long.

Bloom Season: June–September.

Habitat/Range: Waste areas, fields, meadows, and roadsides. Found throughout the region.

Comments: Introduced from Europe, this is one of several yellow clovers in New England.

WITCH HAZEL
Hamamelis virginiana
Witch-Hazel Family (Hamamelidaceae)

Description: This branching shrub can reach a height of up to 20'. The light green leaves are simple, ovate, and 2–6" long. The leaf margins are rimmed with large wavy teeth and have an uneven base. Numerous yellow flowers are found in axillary clusters. The newly emerging buds are hairy in appearance. Individual flowers are about 1" wide with 4 very narrow and very long petals that have a crumpled look to them.

Bloom Season: Mid-September–late October.

Habitat/Range: Woodlands and swamps. Common throughout the region.

Comments: Native Americans treated colds and sore throats with a tea made from the shrub's leaves. A highly astringent tea was prepared from the bark, which is a rich source of tannins useful for treating a wide variety of skin conditions. The branches were often used to make bows and dousing rods to locate underground water. Plant extracts from the leaves, bark, and twigs are widely used today in a number of commercial preparations.

ORANGE DAYLILY
Hemerocallis fulva
Daylily Family (Hemerocallidaceae)

Description: These large, flowering plants range in height from 2–5'. The linear leaves are basal and up to 2½' long, with a smooth margin. The flowers appear in terminal clusters of 3–15. Individual flowers are orange in color, 3–5" wide, and funnel shaped, with 3 recurved petals each with wavy edges.

Bloom Season: June–July.

Habitat/Range: The borders of fields, thickets, and roadsides. Common throughout the region.

Comments: Originally native to Asia, this plant has escaped cultivation in New England. The plant spreads quickly, mainly by rhizomes. In Chinese culture a root tea has been used as a diuretic, and the roots and young shoots have been used to treat mastitis and breast cancer.

PALE ST. JOHN'S WORT
Hypericum ellipticum
St. John's-Wort Family (Hypericaceae)

Description: A branchless plant, 6–20" tall, with a somewhat square stem. The leaves have a smooth margin and are simple, opposite, and elliptic, with rounded ends, ½–1" wide, slightly clasping the stem. The flowers are found at the top of the stem on a branched cluster. Each flower is about ½" wide, with 5 yellow petals, 5 small, pointed sepals, and numerous stamens.

Bloom Season: July–August.

Habitat/Range: Sandy or gravelly shorelines, marshes, bogs, and moist thickets. Found throughout the region.

Comments: A stem decoction was used by Native Americans to suppress menses.

ORANGE-GRASS
Hypericum gentianoides
St. John's-Wort Family (Hypericaceae)

Description: A thinly branched, erect plant averaging 4–18" tall, with a rather wiry appearance. The scale-like leaves are pressed against the stem and reduced. The solitary flower arises in the axils. Individual flowers are ⅛–¼" with 5 yellow petals and 5 linear-shaped sepals that are smaller than the petals.

Bloom Season: July–August.

Habitat/Range: Rocky areas and dry open areas with sandy soil. Found throughout the region to southern Maine.

Comments: The flowers open only in strong sunlight.

DWARF ST. JOHN'S WORT
Hypericum mutilum
St. John's-Wort Family (Hyperiaceae)

Description: This highly branched plant, despite its name, grows 1–3' in height. The common name does not refer to the size of the plant but rather to the size of the flowers. The barely clasping leaves are simple, opposite, oblong to ovate, ½–1½" long, with a rounded base, 3–5 prominent veins, and a smooth margin. There are numerous yellow flowers, ⅛–¼" wide, with 5 petals and 5 sepals that are linear in shape.

Bloom Season: July–August.

Habitat/Range: Wetland areas. Found throughout the region.

Comments: Another small flowered wetlands species is Canada St. John's Wort (*H. canadensis*). The leaves are linear to narrowly ovate and sessile, with 1–3 veins.

COMMON ST. JOHN'S WORT
Hypericum perforatum
St. John's-Wort Family (Hypericaceae)

Description: These plants grow 12–30" tall and are highly branched. The sessile leaves are simple, opposite, linear to oblong, and up to 1½" long with a smooth margin. Many bright yellow flowers are found in terminal clusters. The flower has 5 petals dotted with black spots along the margins. There are 3 styles and numerous stamens.

Bloom Season: Late June–September.

Habitat/Range: Fields, roadsides, and waste areas. Commonly found throughout the region.

Comments: Originally introduced from Europe, this is the most common of the St. John's Wort species found in the region. Ancient Greeks and Romans placed the plant in their homes to protect them from evil spirits, and it was used in the Civil War to treat battle wounds. This plant contains the light-activated toxin hypericin. Many insects avoid foraging on the plant due to the deleterious effects of this phototoxin. Animals grazing on the plant sometimes develop a light-induced dermatitis. Continued feeding on the plant can lead to more severe symptoms such as blistering of the skin, destruction of red blood cells, and, in extreme cases, death. Traditionally this plant has been used in humans to treat mild to moderate forms of depression. However, those taking the plant extract for medical reasons may develop an increased sensitivity to sunlight as a side effect.

SHRUBBY ST. JOHN'S WORT
Hypericum prolificum
St. John's-Wort Family (Hypericaceae)

Description: A shrublike plant, 3–7' tall. The leaves are simple, opposite, oblong to linear shaped, 1–2½" long, and stalked, with a smooth margin. The bright yellow flowers are found, usually 3–7, on terminal racemes. They are ½–1" with 5 petals, 3 styles, and numerous stamens.

Bloom Season: July–August.

Habitat/Range: Woodlands and swamps. Found in widely scattered locales in the region.

Comments: This small shrub produces brown seedpods in September. These pods are often used in dried flower arrangements.

YELLOW STAR-GRASS

Hypoxis hirsuta
Star-Grass Family (Hypoxidaceae)

Description: Grasslike plants, 2–12" tall. The leaves are basal, linear, hairy, and 4–12" long, with a smooth margin and 5–9 veins. On an umbel with a hairy stem are found 2–6 flowers. Individual flowers measure ¾" and are yellow and star shaped, with 3 petals and 3 sepals.

Bloom Season: Late May–early July.

Habitat/Range: Open woodlands and dry meadows. Found in Connecticut, Rhode Island, and Massachusetts to southern Vermont and southern New Hampshire. In Maine it may be extirpated.

Comments: So grasslike are the leaves that when it's not in bloom, this plant can easily be confused with a species of grass.

YELLOW FLAG IRIS

Iris pseudacorus
Iris Family (Iridiaceae)

Description: Yellow Flag Iris ranges in size from 1–3'. The basal leaves are sword shaped and bluish green in color and have a smooth margin. Often taller than the flower stalk, the leaves can measure 18–36" long and less than ¾" wide. The large (3–4") attractive yellow flowers are stalked and terminal, with 3 erect petals and 3 broadly paddle-shaped sepals. The sepals are down turned and marked with purple brown.

Bloom Season: June–early July.

Habitat/Range: Found in wet meadows and marshes and along shorelines. Found scattered throughout the region.

Comments: A European introduction into North America, this plant has escaped cultivation. Once naturalized in the wild, it can form dense clusters that can exclude native wetland species. Caution: Handling the rhizomes and leaves can cause serious skin irritations in sensitive individuals.

COMMON BLADDERWORT
Utricularia macrorhiza
Bladderwort Family (Leutibulariaceae)

Description: These plants are submerged. The leaves are ovate to elliptic, numerous, and ½–2". Each leaf is divided into threadlike segments. Scattered among these leaves are the bladders. There can be upwards to 500 of these saclike bladders per plant. On erect racemes are found 5–15 bright yellow flowers. Individual flowers measure ½–1" with a 3-lobed lower lip.

Bloom Season: July–August.

Habitat/Range: Quiet waters throughout the region.

Comments: A carnivorous plant with bladders that act as tiny traps that capture prey such as tiny crustaceans, protozoans, nematode worms, and occasionally even something as large as a mosquito larva. The traps are hollow and highly transparent and composed of walls only 2 cells thick. A small "door" is situated at the end of the bladder. The door can only swing open in an inward direction. At the front of the door are minute hairs that when touched trigger the door to swing open, sucking in the prey by virtue of a vacuum inside the trap. The door is then quickly reset. The prey is then slowly dissolved by digestive enzymes and absorbed for nutrients. The digestive process takes about 2 hours to complete.

FLOATING BLADDERWORT
Utricularia radiata
Bladderwort Family (Leutibulariaceae)

Description: Floating Bladderwort is a carnivorous aquatic plant lacking a root system. The surface or floating leaves are inflated and found in whorls of 3–8 and have tips that are finely dissected. Scattered along the submerged leaves are numerous tiny bladders. The bladders arise from tiny threadlike segments. The bladders are kidney or pear shaped. The flowers (1–5) are borne on erect racemes. The small flowers are up to ½" wide, yellow in color, and 3 lobed.

Bloom Season: June–July.

Habitat/Range: Ponds. Found throughout most of the region.

Comments: The bladders contain a trap door that is activated by a swimming prey (such as a tiny crustacean) coming in contact with trigger hairs at the bladder's mouth. The prey is probably attracted to sugars secreted by certain specialized cells that reside outside the trap. In less than .01 second, the prey is sucked inside the bladder, where cells begin secreting digestive enzymes. The victim dissolves in a matter of hours, and its remains are absorbed by the plant.

BLUEBEAD LILY
Clintonia borealis
Lily Family (Liliaceae)

Description: These plants grow to 12" tall and have 2–5 bright, shiny basal leaves that are simple, narrowly ovate or ovate, and 4–8" long, with a pointed tip, parallel veins, and smooth margin. On umbels are found 2–8 flowers. Flowers are nodding, loosely bell shaped, greenish yellow to yellow, and up to ¾" long. Each flower has 3 petals, 3 petal-like sepals, 6 bright yellow stamens, and a long green pistil.

Bloom Season: Late May–June.

Habitat/Range: Rich woodlands, thickets, and swamps. Found throughout the region.

Comments: Native Americans used the roots and leaves of this plant to treat a variety of ailments ranging from burns to diabetes. The berries that form are a beautiful blue color. Although believed to be mildly poisonous to humans, the berries are readily eaten by chipmunks.

YELLOW TROUT LILY
Erythronium americanum
Lily Family (Liliaceae)

Description: Plants range from 4–10" and are often found growing in large colonies. The 2 leaves are narrowly ovate or ovate and 1–6" long, with a smooth margin. The light green leaves are speckled with purple-brown markings that are supposed to resemble the speckled coloration of brown trout. The flowers are solitary and nodding, with 3 recurved petals and 3 sepals. The flowers measure 1–2½" in width and are yellow on the inside and brownish on the outside.

Bloom Season: Late April–early May.

Habitat/Range: Rich woodlands, along streams, and in meadows. Commonly found throughout the region.

Comments: One of the region's most common wildflowers. Native Americans brewed a root tea to help bring down fevers. Some Native American women ate the raw leaves in an effort to prevent pregnancy. The young bulbs and leaves can be cooked and eaten as vegetables.

CANADA LILY
Lilium canadense
Lily Family (Liliaceae)

Description: This smooth, erect plant grows 2–6' tall. Leaves are simple and found in whorls of 4–10. Each leaf is lanceolate to narrowly ovate and 3–6" long with a smooth margin. The flowers are found in terminal clusters containing as few as 1 to as many as 15 flowers. Individual flowers are yellow (rarely orange) with dark spots, bell shaped, long stalked, and nodding with 3 slightly recurving petals and 3 petal-like sepals.

Bloom Season: Mid-June–July.

Habitat/Range: Moist meadows and fields. Found throughout the region, although rare in Rhode Island.

Comments: Native Americans treated stomach ailments and rheumatism with a tea prepared from the roots. A root poultice was used as a treatment for snakebites. The roots and flower buds are edible.

TIGER LILY
Lilium lancifolium
Lily Family (Liliaceae)

Description: These erect plants grow 2–5' tall. The leaves are simple and lanceolate, with a smooth margin. Black bulblets are located in the upper leaf axils. The flowers are a reddish orange color spotted with purple on the inside. The flowers are 2–3½" wide, nodding, and found in terminal clusters. The ovate petals are highly recurved. The stamens are protruding.

Bloom Season: Mid-July–August.

Habitat/Range: Meadows, fields, and roadsides. Found scattered throughout the region.

Comments: Tiger Lily is an introduced species now naturalized in the region.

WOOD LILY

Lilium philadelphicum
Lily Family (Liliaceae)

Description: This medium-sized plant grows 1–3' tall. The leaves are simple, whorled, narrowly ovate or ovate, and 2–4" long, with a pointed tip and smooth margin. Unlike most other large lily species, the flowers (1–5 per plant) are upward opening. Individual flowers measure 1½–3". Each reddish orange flower is spotted with purple and has 3 ovate, recurved petals and 3 petal-like sepals.

Bloom Season: Late June–July.

Habitat/Range: Dry woodlands, thickets, and meadows. Found throughout the region north to southern Maine.

Comments: The bulbs were gathered and eaten by Native Americans. A tea was prepared from the roots and used to treat fevers, coughs, and stomach problems. Spider bites were treated with a flower poultice.

TURK'S CAP LILY

Lilium superbum
Lily Family (Liliaceae)

Description: These tall plants can reach a height of 8'. The leaves are found in whorls. Each leaf is ovate and 2–6" long and has a smooth margin. The flowers are found in several terminal clusters, are orange colored and nodding, and measure 2–3½". The ovate petals and petal-like sepals are highly recurved and spotted with purple. A clearly defined star-shaped greenish marking is found at the center of the flower. The stamens are large and conspicuous with dark brown anthers.

Bloom Season: July.

Habitat/Range: Wet woodlands and meadows. Found in Connecticut, Rhode Island, and Massachusetts and into southern New Hampshire.

Comments: Turk's Cap Lily is the largest native lily species found in the United States. Native Americans often prepared a soup from the bulbs.

ROSE MANDARIN
Streptopus lanceolatus
Lily Family (Liliaceae)

Description: These plants, 10–30", grow erect or arching, with a finely hairy stem that grows in a zigzaglike pattern. The leaves, 2–4" long, are primarily lanceolate with conspicuous parallel veins, pointed tip, rounded base, and a smooth margin. The flowers are solitary on a twisted stalk, pinkish purple, and bell shaped, sporting 6 points that are often recurved.

Bloom Season: Mid-May–mid-June.

Habitat/Range: Rich woodlands. Found in Massachusetts, Vermont, New Hampshire, and Maine.

Comments: White Mandarin (*S. amplexifolius*) is similar in appearance and habitat but can be differentiated from *S. lanceolatus* by its greenish white flowers.

WHORLED LOOSESTRIFE
Lysimachia quadrifolia
Myrsine Family (Myrsinaceae)

Description: Plants are 1–3' tall, erect. The leaves are in whorls of 3–6 (most commonly 4), lanceolate, 2–4" long, and sessile, with a smooth margin. The yellow, star-shaped flowers are on a long slender stalk that arises from the leaf axils. The flowers are ½" wide. There are 5 petals, each tinted red at the base and often red-streaked outwards towards the tip. There are 5 stamens and 1 pistil.

Bloom Season: Late June–August.

Habitat/Range: Woodlands, fields, and shorelines. Common throughout the region.

Comments: Native Americans used a leaf tea to treat female, kidney, and bowel ailments.

SWAMP CANDLES
Lysimachia terrestris
Myrsine Family (Myrsinaceae)

Description: An erect plant, 1–3' tall. The leaves are simple, opposite, narrowly ovate, 1–4" long, and sessile, with a smooth margin. Numerous flowers are on terminal racemes that are 2–12" tall. Each flower is ½" wide and yellow, with 5 petals. There are 2 red spots at the base of each petal.

Bloom Season: Mid-June–July.

Habitat/Range: Swamps, marshes, shorelines, and moist ground. Found throughout the region.

Comments: This plant can spread rapidly by underground stems and can form large, dense colonies.

YELLOW POND LILY

Nuphar lutea var. *variegata*
Water-Lily Family (Nymphacaceae)

Description: The leaves of this aquatic plant are floating or occasionally submerged. The leaves are simple, oblong to ovate, and 3–12" wide, with a deep notch at the base and a smooth margin. The upper leaf surface is green while the underside has a reddish coloration. The large bright yellow flowers are solitary, with 6 petal-like sepals, and measure 3–5" in width. The flower rests at or slightly above the water surface.

Bloom Season: Mid-June–August.

Habitat/Range: Ponds and lakes. Found throughout the region.

Comments: Native Americans made a tea from the roots, used to treat a host of ailments ranging from blood diseases to boils.

EVENING PRIMROSE

Oenothera biennis
Evening-Primrose Family (Onagraceae)

Description: A branching, hairy plant, 1–8' in height. The leaves are simple, alternate, ovate to lanceolate, sessile or short stalked, and 4–8" long, with a slightly toothed margin. The flowers are on terminal spikes. Individual flowers are yellow, 1–2" wide, with 4 rounded petals, 4 recurved sepals, and an X-shaped stigma.

Bloom Season: Early July–early September.

Habitat/Range: Weedy areas, fields, and roadsides. Found throughout the region.

Comments: The flowers open in the evening and close by the next morning. Moths are the most common pollinators. Native Americans treated obesity and bowel problems with a tea made from the plant's roots. All parts of the plant are edible. The flowers and leaves can be added to salads while the roots, rich in magnesium and potassium, can be boiled and eaten. The seeds have even been used as a substitute for poppy seeds. The plant is also a good natural source of gamma-linolenic acid, an essential fatty acid required in the human diet.

LARGE YELLOW LADY'S SLIPPER

Cypripedium parviflorum var. *pubescens*
Orchid Family (Orchidaceae)

Description: This showy member of the Orchid Family can grow to a height of 30" and is hairy. The leaves are simple, alternate, lanceolate to ovate, pointed at the tip, and up to 8" long, with a smooth margin. There are 3–5 leaves on each plant. The leaves are clasping the stem and are conspicuously parallel veined. Usually 1–2 terminal flowers are found on the stalk. The lateral petals are very narrow, pointed, up to 3" in length, yellowish green to brown, and usually found twisted into a loose corkscrewlike fashion. The lip petal is yellow, pouchlike, inflated, and up to 2" long. There are 2 yellowish green sepals positioned above and below the lip petal.

Bloom Season: Mid-May–mid-June.

Habitat/Range: Moist woodlands, swamps, fens, and bogs. Found scattered throughout the region.

Comments: Over the last quarter of a century, this species' numbers have declined significantly in the region in large part due to overcollecting. A less hairy and slightly smaller variety, Small Yellow Lady's Slipper (*C. parviflorum* var. *mokasin*) can be distinguished from *C. parviflorum* var. *pubescens* by its smaller lip petal and by the deeper purple coloration of its lateral petals and sepals.

YELLOW-FRINGED ORCHID

Platanthera ciliaris
Orchid Family (Orchidaceae)

Description: This orchid stands 12–30" tall. The basal leaves number 1–3. Each leaf is narrowly ovate and 4–10" long and has a smooth margin. The upper leaves are smaller. The flowers are crowded on spikes measuring 3–8" tall. Individual flowers are yellowish orange in color and measure ½" wide. Sepals are ¼" and ovate. The lateral petals appear ragged edged or torn. The deeply fringed oblong lip petal is ½–¾" long and has a spur measuring up to 1½" long.

Bloom Season: Late July–August.

Habitat/Range: Open woodlands, fields, thickets, dry meadows, and occasionally bogs. In New England the species is currently limited to a few sites in Connecticut and Rhode Island. Southern New England is pretty much the northern limit for the distribution of this orchid.

Comments: This very showy member of the orchid family has become a regionally important species. The loss of habitat has greatly reduced its numbers. It was last reported in Massachusetts more than 30 years ago.

DOWNY FALSE FOXGLOVE
Aureolaria virginica
Broom-Rape Family (Orobanchaceae)

Description: Plants are 1–5' tall with a downy stem. The lower leaves are simple, opposite, downy, narrowly ovate or ovate, 2–5" long, often lobed, and stalked, with a pointed tip. The upper leaves are similar but smaller. The flowers are found in a terminal cluster with a single flower in the axil of each opposite bract. The flowers are bright yellow, 1¼–1½" long, and short stalked, with a funnel-shaped 5-lobed corolla and 4 stamens.

Bloom Season: July–early August.

Habitat/Range: Dry oak woodlands. Found scattered throughout the southern portion of the region.

Comments: This species is hemi-parasitic on the roots of oak trees.

YELLOW WOOD SORREL
Oxalis stricta
Wood-Sorrel Family (Oxalidaceae)

Description: These erect, hairy-stemmed plants grow 6–18". The stem color can range from green to purple. The leaves are alternate, long-stalked, and cloverlike, divided into 3 leaflets. The leaflets are heart shaped and hairless, measuring up to ¾" wide, with a smooth margin. The leaflets close at night. One to several flowers are found on umbels. The flowers are yellow with 5 rounded petals.

Bloom Season: May–August.

Habitat/Range: Dry open areas, fields, roadsides, and waste areas. Common throughout the region.

Comments: Although the leaves have frequently been eaten in salads, they are somewhat sour tasting due to their high oxalic acid content.

CELANDINE

Chelidonium majus
Poppy Family (Papaveraceae)

Description: Celandine grows 3–24" tall and contains an orange sap. The leaves are alternate and divided into 5–7 lobes, with each lobe up to 3" long. A few yellow flowers are found on umbels. The flowers have 4 rounded petals, each ½–¾" wide, and 2 sepals that drop off during flowering.

Bloom Season: Mid-May–June.

Habitat/Range: Woodland edges and areas of rich soils. Found throughout the region.

Comments: Originally from Europe. The sap can cause severe skin irritations in sensitive people.

BUTTER-AND-EGGS

Linaria vulgaris
Plantain Family (Plantaginaceae)

Description: This European introduction can grow to 3' tall. The leaves are simple, alternate, linear (almost grasslike), and ½–2" long, with a smooth margin. The flowers are found on crowded terminal racemes. Individual flowers are yellow, ¾–1", tubular in appearance, and 2 lipped. A long spur and a prominent orange ridge are found on the lower lip.

Bloom Season: Mid-June–August.

Habitat/Range: Fields, roadsides, and waste areas. Common throughout the region.

Comments: Butter-and-Eggs reproduces both by seeds and by creeping rhizomes. The plant's root system can form extensive colonies that often outcompete native species. A leaf tea historically was used to treat ailments such as jaundice and piles. It was also frequently used as a laxative and as a diuretic. Alkaloids found in the plant are considered mildly to moderately toxic to livestock. The plant has been used to control erosion and to reclaim land contaminated by heavy metals.

MARSH MARIGOLD
Caltha palustris
Crowfoot Family (Ranunculaceae)

Description: Plants are leafy, possess a hollow succulent stem, and grow to 2' in height. The basal leaves are round to kidney shaped, 1–6" long, stalked, and notched at the base, usually with a finely toothed margin. The upper leaves are smaller and sessile. The bright glossy yellow-stalked flowers are 1–1½" wide with 5–9 petal-like sepals and buttercuplike in appearance. Petals are absent.

Bloom Season: Late April–May.

Habitat/Range: Swamps, bogs, along streams and brooks, ponds, and wet meadows. Common throughout the region.

Comments: One of the first flowers to appear in the early spring. The main pollinators are flies and beetles. The flowers were sometimes boiled and used to dye yarn. The leaves, rich in iron, were boiled by Native Americans and used to treat anemia. In addition, Native Americans made a tea from the leaves that acted as a laxative and diuretic. A root tea was used as an emetic and expectorant. The plant can cause skin irritation in sensitive individuals. The raw plant cannot be eaten and is particularly poisonous to livestock. The active compounds are the alkaloid jervine and the glucoside helleborin.

HISPID BUTTERCUP
Ranunculus hispidus
Crowfoot Family (Ranunculaceae)

Description: A branching, hairy plant, 1–3' tall. The basal leaves are palmately divided into 3–7 segments. Leaves are 1–4" long and stalked. The upper leaves are reduced in size. The golden yellow flowers are up to 1½" wide with 5–8 petals and 5 hairy sepals that are shorter than the petals.

Bloom Season: Mid-May–mid-June.

Habitat/Range: Found in fields, woodlands, swamps, and marshes throughout the region.

Comments: The stem and leaves contain an extremely acrid sap.

HOOKED CROWFOOT
Ranunculus recurvatus
Crowfoot Family (Ranunculaceae)

Description: This common member of the Crowfoot Family (sometimes referred to as the Buttercup Family) ranges in height from 6–24" and is hairy. The stalked leaves are simple, alternate, kidney shaped, and 1–4" long, with 3–5 lobes. There are only a few stem leaves. The flowers are yellow and individually stalked and measure approximately ¼". There are 5 rounded petals, 5 short, recurved sepals, and numerous stamens.

Bloom Season: Mid-May–June.

Habitat/Range: Woodlands and streams. Found throughout the region.

Comments: Native Americans used root preparations to alleviate toothaches and as a laxative.

WOODLAND AGRIMONY
Agrimonia striata
Rose Family (Rosaceae)

Description: Plants grow 2–4' tall. The leaves are alternate, pinnately compound, and divided into 7–11 leaflets, each of which is narrowly ovate, 1–2" long, slightly hairy, and coarsely toothed. The flowers are on crowded spikes. Each ¼" flower has 5 yellow petals, 5 green sepals, and a base that is surrounded by a series of hooked green bristles.

Bloom Season: August–early September.

Habitat/Range: Open woodlands, thickets, and roadsides. Found throughout the region to southern Maine.

Comments: Whole plant preparations were used in folk medicine as a mouthwash.

SHRUBBY CINQUEFOIL
Dasiphora fruticosa
Rose Family (Rosaceae)

Description: A shrubby plant 1–3' tall. The leaves are alternate, pinnately compound, being divided into 5–7 leaflets, each being narrowly ovate to lanceolate, broader at either end, and ½–¾" long, with a smooth margin. The upper leaf surface is green; the lower, whitish in color. The flowers are mostly solitary, terminal, ¾–1¼" wide, and bright yellow with 5 rounded petals.

Bloom Season: Mid-June–July.

Habitat/Range: Along shorelines, moist meadows, and bogs. Found throughout the region.

Comments: *D. fruticosa* is a frequently cultivated shrub.

ROUGH CINQUEFOIL
Potentilla norvegica
Rose Family (Rosaceae)

Description: Plants, branching and hairy, grow 1–3' tall. The leaves are alternate and divided into 3 leaflets. Each leaflet is elliptic to ovate in shape and up to 3" long with a toothed margin. The flowers, several to many, are terminal, yellow, and ¼–⅜" wide, with 5 rounded petals and 5 green sepals that are slightly longer than the petals.

Bloom Season: Late June–July.

Habitat/Range: Thickets, clearings, and roadsides. Found throughout the region.

Comments: Considered by many to be a weedy species.

ROUGH-FRUITED CINQUEFOIL
Potentilla recta
Rose Family *(Rosaceae)*

Description: A nonbranching plant that grows 1–2' tall and is hairy. The compound leaves are palmately divided into 5 or 6 leaflets. Each leaflet is narrowly ovate, 1–6" long, and broader towards the tip, with a toothed margin. The flowers are on a flat-topped panicle. Each flower is ½–1" wide and light yellow in color, with 5 notched petals, 5 smaller sepals, and numerous pistils and stamens.

Bloom Season: Late June–mid-August.

Habitat/Range: Dry fields, weedy areas, and roadsides. Found throughout the region.

Comments: A native of Eurasia, this species is considered a serious weed pest in the midwestern United States.

COMMON CINQUEFOIL
Potentilla simplex
Rose Family (Rosaceae)

Description: These plants are erect or arching and ½–4', with hairy stems and the ability to form runners. The alternate leaves are palmately compound, with 5 leaflets that are elliptic to lanceolate and ½–3" long, with a toothed margin. The solitary flowers arise from the leaf axils on a long stem. They are bright yellow and up to ½" wide with 5 rounded petals and 5 sepals.

Bloom Season: May–July.

Habitat/Range: Found in dry woodlands, fields, and roadsides especially in nutrient-poor soils. Common throughout the region.

Comments: In general, cinquefoils are high in tannins although the young shoots and leaves can be eaten as salad greens.

PUSSY WILLOW

Salix discolor
Willow Family (Salicaceae)

Description: A medium-sized shrub, 3–16' tall, with catkins that are furrylike and appear before the leaves begin to emerge. The leaves are lanceolate, with a smooth or nearly smooth margin. The leaves are bright green on the upper surface and greenish white on the underside. The male and female flowers are on separate catkins. The catkins containing the male flowers are yellow and up to 2" long. The catkin that contains the greenish female flowers are up to 2½" long.

Bloom Season: Mid-February–late April.

Habitat/Range: Thickets, swamps, and streambeds. Found throughout the region.

Comments: As seen with other willow species, this plant contains salicin and was used by Native Americans as a painkiller.

NORTHERN PITCHER PLANT

Sarracenia purpurea
Pitcher-Plant Family (Sarraceniaceae)

Description: This carnivorous plant species has basal leaves that have been modified to form a tubular structure resulting in a pitcherlike appearance. The pitchers are greenish red, with purplish, veinlike markings, and 4–10" long. There is a flared-out top lip partially covering the pitcher that is covered on the inside with short, sharp downward-pointing hairs. The large solitary flowers are borne above the leaves on a long stalk 10–18" tall. The flower is reddish purple with a yellowish center and measures up to 2" in width. There are 5 petals present.

Bloom Season: Mid-June–July.

Habitat/Range: Peat bogs, sandy shorelines, and, occasionally, wet meadows. Found throughout the region.

Comments: Insects entering the pitcher often find themselves trapped in the pool of water at the bottom. The numerous downward-pointing spines lining the inside of the pitcher make it problematic for the insect to get back out. The unfortunate victim usually drowns and is digested by enzymes secreted by the plant into the water. Native Americans used the roots to treat lung and liver ailments and also to treat smallpox.

COMMON MULLEIN

Verbascum thapsus
Scroph Family (Scrophulariaceae)

Description: Plants are erect, 2–8' tall, and densely woolly. The pale gray-green leaves are simple and alternate. The lower leaves are oblong to ovate, 4–12" long, densely hairy, and stalked, with a smooth or toothed margin. The upper leaves are smaller and sessile. Numerous flowers are on an erect spike, 4–20" tall, which is occasionally found branched. The yellow flowers are tubular, up to 1" wide, with 5 rounded petals and 5 sepals.

Bloom Season: June–September.

Habitat/Range: Fields, roadsides, and a variety of weedy areas throughout the region.

Comments: Originally from Europe. The flowers and leaves have been used in folk medicine to treat many different ailments including coughs, earaches, and kidney infections. Also used in European folklore to ward off witches. Women used the bright yellow dye produced from boiling the flowers to color both clothing and hair. The seeds are considered a favorite snack of the American Goldfinch, believed to be the only bird that will regularly feed on mullein.

DOWNY YELLOW VIOLET

Viola pubescens
Violet Family (Violaceae)

Description: This violet reaches a height up to 16" and is lightly hairy. There are 2–4 heart-shaped leaves on long stalks, with a toothed margin. Flowers and leaves are on the same stalk. The flowers are axillary and ½–¾" wide, with 5 yellow petals that are marked with brownish purple veins. The 2 lateral petals are hairy inside.

Bloom Season: May.

Habitat/Range: Rich woodlands and meadows. Found throughout the region.

Comments: Native Americans took a plant decoction for indigestion.

185

NORTHERN YELLOW-EYED GRASS
Xyris montana
Yellow-Eyed-Grass Family (Xyridaceae)

Description: Small, delicate plants measuring up to 12". The dark green, grasslike leaves are basal, simple, linear, and 2–6" long, with flattened sides, a reddish base, and smooth margin. One to a few flowers are borne on slender spikes. The flowers are yellow and ¼", with 3 petal-like lobes. The sepals are folded with the central crease (keel) only slightly ragged towards the tip. The flower opens in the morning.

Bloom Season: Late June–July.

Habitat/Range: Bogs, swamps, and wet, sandy soils. Found throughout the region.

Comments: Difficult group to identify without relying on the characteristics of the sepals.

BLUE AND PURPLE FLOWERS

Flowers in this section range from pale
blue to indigo and pale lavender to maroon
to deep violet. Pale colors could grade into
white and pink. One should also check the
white section and the pink and red section
of the book.

COMMON PERIWINKLE
Vinca minor
Dogbane Family (Apocynaceae)

Description: Periwinkle is a trailing evergreen up to 3' long. The shiny leaves are simple, opposite, oblong, and 1–2" long with a pointed tip and a smooth margin. The solitary flowers arising in the leaf axils are ¾–1" wide and blue-violet (rarely pink or white) in color. The tube-shaped corolla has 5 lobes and a whitish star at its center.

Bloom Season: Late April–May.

Habitat/Range: Woodlands, meadows, and roadsides. Found throughout the region to southern Maine.

Comments: Escaped from cultivation. This plant spreads mainly by underground runners and by rootlets formed at the leaf nodes and can often be found growing in large patches.

COMMON BURDOCK
Arctium minus
Composite Family (Asteraceae)

Description: Plants are erect, bushy, 2–5' tall, with a hollow stem that is hairy and grooved. The leaves are simple, alternate, egg shaped, and 4–18" long, with hollow leaf stalks and a toothed or wavy margin. The leaves are dark green on the upper surface and woolly and light green underneath. The thistlelike flower heads are found on elongated racemes in the upper leaf axils. The heads are a pink-lavender color, prickly, stalkless or very short stalked, and ½–1" wide. The heads lack ray flowers but have numerous tubular disk flowers.

Bloom Season: July–August.

Habitat/Range: Roadsides, weedy places, and old fields. Common throughout the region.

Comments: Introduced into North America by the early colonists. Common Burdock became a widespread weed by the early 1700s and was a valuable resource. Paper was made from the fibers of the inner stem, and a coffee substitute was derived from the dried roots. It was also used to treat a variety of ailments. The spiny burs, which readily attach to clothing, in 1950 provided the inspiration for the invention of Velcro. Common Burdock grows rapidly and is an aggressive colonizer of disturbed soils, often forming large, dense colonies that quickly can outcompete native species.

SPOTTED KNAPWEED
Centaurea biebersteinii
Composite Family (Asteraceae)

Description: Plants grow 1–4' and are highly branched. The wiry stems are gray-green in color. The lower leaves are deeply lobed. As the leaves ascend the stem they become smaller and less lobed. The individual leaflets are linear and 2–8" long and become smaller and less dissected as they grow upward on the stem. The leaves along the flower stalks are grayish green. The lavender (occasionally pink or white) flower heads are solitary, ½–1" wide, and rayless and are found at the ends of branches and in leaf axils. The outer flowers of the head are not significantly enlarged compared to inner flowers, but they are sterile. The involucral bracts are black tipped and fringed with hairs.

Bloom Season: July–August.

Habitat/Range: Fields, weedy areas, and roadsides. Found throughout the region to central Maine.

Comments: This European introduction readily colonizes disturbed ground, outcompeting native species and reducing plant diversity as a consequence. It does this by releasing into the soil polyphenolic flavonoids known collectively as catechins. Catechins can adversely affect the growth of other species and can be recalcitrant in soils for prolonged periods of time.

BROWN KNAPWEED
Centaurea jacea
Composite Family (Asteraceae)

Description: Plants are 8–40" with light green foliage. The basal leaves are elliptic and 4–6" long, sometimes with small lobes. The stem leaves are smaller and narrowly ovate, with a smooth margin. The flower heads are solitary, ¾–1½" wide and violet (or rarely white) and have outer flowers that are larger than the others.

Bloom Season: July–September.

Habitat/Range: Fields, roadsides, and weedy areas. Found throughout the region.

Comments: This Eurasian introduction is aggressive and highly invasive.

WILD CHICORY
Cichorium intybus
Composite Family (Asteraceae)

Description: A loosely branched plant, 1–4' tall, with a stiff stem and milky sap. Lower leaves are simple, alternate, elliptic or ovate, and 3–8" long, with a toothed or lobed margin, giving them a dandelion-like appearance. Upper leaves are reduced in size and clasp the stem. Found in the axils of the upper leaves are 1–3 flower heads. Flower heads are approximately 1½" in diameter, sessile, and composed of blue (rarely white) petal-like rays with toothed edges and dark blue anthers. Heads are composed exclusively of ray flowers. Only 1 flower head in a cluster will bloom at a time.

Bloom Season: Mid-June–September.

Habitat/Range: Fields, roadsides, and waste areas. Commonly found throughout the region.

Comments: Flowers last only 1 day and open only a few at a time. The flower opens early in the morning and closes around noon. Now naturalized in the region, it was originally a European import. The roots and leaves were used in European folk medicine to treat ailments ranging from jaundice to liver problems. It was also favored as a diuretic and laxative. Wild Chicory is sometimes grown as a crop plant. In Europe it is grown in small amounts as a vegetable and salad crop. The roots are often dried and ground and used as a coffee additive or as a substitute for coffee. The roots also contain high levels of the carbohydrate inulin. Inulin is increasingly being used in the food industry as a sweetener and bulking agent. Humans cannot fully digest the complex carbohydrate, and this aids in reducing an individual's caloric intake. High levels of inulin are also found in dandelion roots.

BIG-LEAVED ASTER
Eurybia macrophylla
Composite Family (Asteraceae)

Description: Plants are 1–2½' tall with ovate to heart-shaped leaves that are 2–12" long, stalked or sessile, and sometimes hairy, with a toothed margin. The lower leaves have a rough feel to them. The flower heads are on flat-topped panicles, the branches of which have tiny gland-tipped hairs. Individual flower heads are ½–1¼" wide with 10–20 pale lavender rays surrounding a yellow central disk. Involucral bracts are rounded to somewhat pointed.

Bloom Season: Late June–July.

Habitat/Range: Woodlands. Found throughout the region.

Comments: A nearly identical-looking species, *E. shreberi*, occurs in the region in similar habitats. It has flower heads with rays that are always white while those of *E. macrophylla* are usually lavender. In addition, the gland-tipped hairs are absent.

SHOWY ASTER
Eurybia spectabilis
Composite Family (Asteraceae)

Description: Plants are 1–2' tall with a stiff, weakly branching and hairy stem at the top. The lower stem leaves are lanceolate and 2–5" long, with a pointed tip and slightly toothed margin with either a rough or smooth texture. The upper stem leaves are reduced, linear or oblong, and sessile, with a smooth margin. The flower heads are on open flat-topped panicles. Each head is ¾–1½" wide with a yellow central disk surrounded by 15–30 violet rays. The involucral bracts are oblong shaped with spreading tips.

Bloom Season: Early September–early October.

Habitat/Range: Dry sandy soils especially those found in pine-dominated areas. Found in scattered locations in eastern Massachusetts, eastern Connecticut, and Rhode Island.

Comments: Considered an endangered species in Connecticut.

STIFF ASTER
Ionactis linariifolius
Composite Family (Asteraceae)

Description: These asters are short stemmed and stiff, ranging from 4–18" in height. The dark green leaves are linear, ½–1½" long, pointed at the tip, and sessile, with a smooth margin. One to several heads are found on flat-topped panicles. The pale blue-violet heads are ½–1" wide and have a yellow central disk surrounded by 10–20 rays. Small leafy bracts are on the flower stalks.

Bloom Season: Mid-August–early October.

Habitat/Range: Thrives mainly in dry, open areas and favors those with sandy-type soils. Found throughout the region to central Maine.

Comments: The common name is derived from the relatively stiff stem and leaves characteristic of this species.

TALL BLUE LETTUCE
Lactuca biennis
Composite Family (Asteraceae)

Description: Plants erect, 2–6' tall, with a milky sap. Leaves are simple, alternate, elliptic, stalked, highly lobed or with a toothed margin, and 4–10" long and appear dandelion-like. Found on narrow crowded panicles are 15–30 blue flower heads. Each head measures ½–¾" wide with 10–18 rays.

Bloom Season: July–September.

Habitat/Range: Woodlands, clearings, and thickets. Found throughout the region.

Comments: Native Americans applied the sap to pimples and made a tea from the roots to treat nausea, pain, and diarrhea. Sensitive individuals may develop a dermatitis from coming into contact with the sap.

NEW ENGLAND ASTER
Symphyotrichum novae-angliae
Composite Family (Asteraceae)

Description: Large leafy plants with a hairy stem. The leaves are simple, alternate, lanceolate, 1–4" long, pointed at the tip, and hairy, with a smooth margin, and clasp the stem. Several to many flower heads are found on short panicles. Each head measures ¾–1½" wide and is a dark violet to bluish purple. The flower head is composed of a yellow central disk surrounded by 30–50 rays (on average, although the number could be as much as 80–100). Involucral bracts have very broadly pointed or blunt tips.

Bloom Season: August–October.

Habitat/Range: Thickets, meadows, fields, moist open areas, and swamps. Found throughout the region.

Comments: Native Americans made a root tea from this showy aster to treat diarrhea and fevers.

CLASPING ASTER
Symphyotrichum patens
Composite Family (Asteraceae)

Description: Plants are 1–3' tall with a rough, hairy stem. The leaves clasp the stem and are oblong to ovate, 1–6" long, and hairy, with a pointed tip, notched base, and smooth margin. The flower heads are found on panicles. Each head is ½–1" wide and has a yellow central disk and 15–30 light purple rays. The involucral bracts are narrow and pointed.

Bloom Season: August–October.

Habitat/Range: Dry open areas in woodlands and fields. Found in Connecticut, Rhode Island, and Massachusetts to central Vermont, New Hampshire, and extreme southern Maine.

Comments: This species is on the threatened list in New Hampshire and may be extirpated in Maine.

NEW YORK IRONWEED

Vernonia noveboracencis
Composite Family (Asteraceae)

Description: An erect plant, 2–7' tall, and branching near the top of the stem. The leaves are simple, alternate, and 3–10" long, with a pointed tip and with a finely toothed margin. Numerous flower heads are found on loose, flat-topped panicles. Each head is purple in color, up to ⅝" wide, and rayless.

Bloom Season: August–October.

Habitat/Range: Fields, wet woodlands, marshes, and stream banks. Found throughout Connecticut, Rhode Island, and Massachusetts to extreme southern Vermont and New Hampshire.

Comments: Native Americans used a root tea to help regulate menses, relieve pain after childbirth, control bleeding, and calm stomachaches.

VIRGINIA BLUEBELLS

Mertensia virginica
Borage Family (Boraginaceae)

Description: An erect plant, 8–24", with blue-green foliage. The basal leaves are 2–6" long, narrowly ovate or ovate, rounded or pointed at the end, and with a smooth margin. The stem leaves are similar but smaller. The flowers are on racemes. Each blue flower is ½–1" long, trumpet shaped, nodding, with a 5-lobed corolla.

Bloom Season: Mid-April–May.

Habitat/Range: Moist woodlands and clearings. Virginia Bluebells is a rare plant in New England. Its distribution is limited to a few locales in Maine and Massachusetts.

Comments: Native Americans used a root preparation to treat venereal disease.

GARDEN FORGET-ME-NOT
Myosotis sylvatica
Borage Family (Boraginaceae)

Description: These plants are hairy and grow to 16" in height. The leaves are narrowly ovate to oblong, 1–2" long, sessile, and hairy. The stalked flowers are found on racemes. Flowers are light blue with a yellow center, 5 petals, and a hairy calyx.

Bloom Season: May–early June.

Habitat/Range: Found along woodland edges and fields throughout the region.

Comments: Originally from Europe, this garden escape has naturalized throughout New England. The native Small Forget-Me-Not (*M. laxa*) has a very similar appearance but with smaller (⅛") flowers.

DAME'S ROCKET
Hesperis matronalis
Mustard Family (Brassicaceae)

Description: Plants erect, 2–4' tall. Leaves are simple, opposite, 3–8" long, and sessile, with a pointed tip and toothed margin. Numerous fragrant flowers are found on racemes. Each flower is ½–¾" wide and purple, pink, or white. Four rounded petals and 4 sepals are present.

Bloom Season: Late May–June.

Habitat/Range: Woodland edges, thickets, and roadsides. Found throughout the region.

Comments: Originally a European garden plant, Dame's Rocket has now naturalized throughout much of North America.

CREEPING BELLFLOWER
Campanula rapunculoides
Bellflower Family (Campanulaceae)

Description: This introduced species grows 1–3' tall, with simple, alternate leaves that are ovate to nearly elliptic and 2–4" long, with an irregularly toothed margin. Numerous flowers are found on one-sided racemes. Each flower is ¾–1¼" long, blue-purple, and bell shaped, with 5 lobes and narrow sepals.

Bloom Season: Mid-July–early October.

Habitat/Range: Fields, roadsides, and waste areas. Found throughout the region.

Comments: Reproduces by both seed and a white, creeping root and as a result often forms dense stands that can outcompete native species.

SPIKED LOBELIA
Lobelia spicata
Bellflower Family (Campanulaceae)

Description: These plants grow 12–36" tall and have a stem that is hairy at the base and smooth above. The basal leaves are simple, alternate, ovate or round, 2–4", and stalked, with a smooth margin. The upper leaves are reduced and sessile. Many pale blue flowers are found on an erect slender spike. Each is ¼–⅜" and 2 lipped with a 2-lobed upper lip and 3-lobed lower.

Bloom Season: Late June–August.

Habitat/Range: Woodlands, fields, meadows, and thickets. Found throughout the region.

Comments: Native Americans used both the roots and leaves for a variety of medicinal purposes.

VENUS'S LOOKING GLASS
Triodanis perfoliata
Bellflower Family (Campanulaceae)

Description: These sparsely branched plants are erect, 4–18" tall, and hairy along the lower portion, with a milky sap. The leaves clasp the stem and are simple, alternate, ovate to shell shaped, with a scalloped margin, and ½–1" wide. The flowers are found singly in the leaf axils. They are blue-violet in color and ¾" long, and have a corolla with 5 widely spreading lobes and triangular sepals.

Bloom Season: Mid-May–August.

Habitat/Range: Dry woodlands, fields, and disturbed sites. Found throughout the region to southern Maine.

Comments: The flowers that form in the lower axils do not open but do produce seed.

ASIATIC DAYFLOWER
Commelina communis
Spiderwort Family (Commelinaceae)

Description: These leafy plants grow 6–30" long, are creeping, and have leaves that sheath the stem. The sessile leaves are simple, alternate, narrowly ovate, and 2–5" long, with a rounded base, pointed tip, and smooth margin. The leaf surfaces are often hairy. The flowers are solitary, ½–1" long. A round bract measuring ½–1" surrounds each flower. Each flower has 3 green sepals, 3 petals, and 6 stamens. The lower petal is small and whitish while the 2 upper petals are larger, rounded, and deep blue in color.

Bloom Season: June–September.

Habitat/Range: Weedy areas, disturbed sites, and roadsides. Found in Connecticut, Rhode Island, and Massachusetts to southern Vermont, southern New Hampshire, and southeastern Maine.

Comments: Introduced from Asia, the flowers of this plant only open for 1 day. The plant often forms dense colonies because of its ability to root from stem nodes. This plant is considered a medicinal herb in China.

WILD LUPINE
Lupinus perennis
Bean Family (Fabaceae)

Description: These erect plants grow 6–24" tall and are marginally hairy. The leaves are alternate, pinnately compound with individual leaflets narrowly ovate, wider at the tip, ¾–3" in length, and long stalked, with a smooth margin. The flowers are found on terminal racemes that measure 4–8" tall. The flowers are blue, pink, or white. Each flower is ½–¾" long and pea-like in appearance.

Bloom Season: May–June.

Habitat/Range: Dry open woodlands, fields, and clearings. Found throughout the region but scarce in Maine.

Comments: The seeds of this native species are poisonous. Native Americans prepared a leaf tea that was used to treat nausea and to help control internal hemorrhaging. Aids soil fertility by virtue of its nitrogen-fixing ability, as is the case with most members of the Bean Family.

COW VETCH
Vicia cracca
Bean Family (Fabaceae)

Description: Cow Vetch is a trailing or climbing plant, 2–3' long, and hairy. The leaves are alternate, pinnately compound, and divided into 12–24 leaflets. Each leaflet is about 1" long and lanceolate, with a pointed tip and smooth margin. In addition, a pair of tendrils is located at the end of each leaf. On average there are 20–50 bluish purple flowers located on a 1-sided raceme. Individual flowers are ¼–½" long and curve downward on a long stalk.

Bloom Season: Mid-May–August.

Habitat/Range: Fields, meadows, and roadsides. Found throughout the region.

Comments: This Eurasian climbing vine can often shade out other native species in areas where it grows in large colonies.

CLOSED GENTIAN
Gentiana clausa
Gentian Family (Gentiaceae)

Description: Plants are 6–24" tall. The leaves directly below the flower cluster are arranged in a whorl while those farther down the stem are simple, opposite, narrowly ovate or ovate, and 2–4" long, with a smooth margin. The flowers are found in a cluster atop the stem. Each is a blue-violet color, cylindrical in shape, and 1–1½" long, with a corolla with 5 fused lobes that are closed at the tip.

Bloom Season: August–early October.

Habitat/Range: Woodlands, thickets, and meadows. Found throughout the region to southern Maine.

Comments: Bottle Gentian, *G. andrewsii,* is nearly identical in appearance to *G. clausa* except that the tip of the flower is more tightly closed and there are fringed edges between all the lobes. Populations of gentians have been steadily decreasing due to loss of wetland habitats.

WILD GERANIUM
Geranium maculatum
Geranium Family (Geraniaceae)

Description: These native plants grow up to 2'
tall. There are several hairy leaves that are
dissected into 5–7 deep lobes. The leaves are
alternate, measure 3–5" long, and have a toothed
margin. Several to many flowers are found in a
loose cluster. Individual flowers are purple to
purple-rose, and 1–1½" wide with 5 rounded
petals and 5 pointed sepals that are
characteristically shorter than the petals.

Bloom Season: Mid-May–June.

Habitat/Range: Woodlands, thickets, and
meadows. Commonly found in the southern part
of the region.

Comments: Native Americans used root
preparations as a means to stop bleeding and
diarrhea and to treat stomach ailments. The roots
are rich in tannins, which can account for up to 20
percent of the dry weight of the roots.

SLENDER BLUE FLAG IRIS
Iris prismatica
Iris Family (Iridaceae)

Description: The plant's flower stem averages
12–36" tall. The long, sword-shaped, pale green
leaves measure up to 24" long, are less than ½"
in diameter, and have smooth margins. One to 3
violet-blue flowers are found on the erect stem.
Each flower measures 2–3" wide with 3 erect
petals and 3 spreading or downward-turned
sepals that are usually veined with dark purple.

Bloom Season: June–early July.

Habitat/Range: Swamps, wet meadows, and
marshes. Found in Connecticut, Rhode Island, and
eastern Massachusetts to northern New
Hampshire.

Comments: Similar to Northern Blue Flag Iris (*I.
versicolor*) but this plant's leaves rarely exceed ½"
in diameter. Also the seed capsule is strongly
angular.

NORTHERN BLUE FLAG IRIS

Iris versicolor

Iris Family (Iridaceae)

Description: These plants have stems measuring 6–30" in height. The pale green basal leaves are sword shaped, 6–30" long, and ½–1" wide, with smooth margins. Each plant bears several stalked flowers, each 2–4" wide and violet-blue in color. Individual flowers have 3 erect petals and 3 down-turned, spreading sepals. Flower production does not occur until the second or third year of growth. Sepals often have a greenish yellow spot at their base. Bluish veins mark a white background that surrounds the base of the sepals.

Bloom Season: June–early July.

Habitat/Range: Meadows, swamps, marshes, and other wet shorelines. Found throughout the region.

Comments: Although poisonous, the rhizomes were used by Native Americans in small amounts as a cathartic and diuretic. The main toxic component is the resinoid irisin.

BLUE-EYED GRASS

Sisyrinchium angustifolium

Iris Family (Iridaceae)

Description: Plants grow 6–18" and have a winged stem and grasslike foliage. The leaves are basal, simple, linear, ⅛–¼" wide, and 6–20" long, with a smooth margin. The light blue-violet flowers, 1–3, are terminal and ½–¾" long with 6 rounded or notched petals and a yellow center and have an overall star-shaped appearance.

Bloom Season: Mid-May–June.

Habitat/Range: Moist woodlands, meadows, and stream banks. Found throughout the region.

Comments: Native Americans treated children's diarrhea with a root tea preparation and used a plant tea to expel worms. A leaf tea was used to treat stomach ailments.

CARPET BUGLEWEED

Ajuga reptans
Mint Family (Lamiaceae)

Description: Plants grow 6–12" tall. The stem is erect and hairy. The leaves are simple, opposite, ovate, purple or coppery in color, and 1–2½" long, with a smooth or toothed margin. The blue flowers are found in loose spikes. Each flower is about ½" long. The corolla is tubular and 2 lipped. The upper lip is shorter than the lower. The lower lip is 3 lobed.

Bloom Season: May–June.

Habitat/Range: Moist woodlands, gardens, and lawns. Common throughout the southern parts of New England. Its distribution is spotty in northern New England.

Comments: This species is native to Europe. The whole plant is used as an astringent in herbal medicine practices.

WILD BASIL

Clinopodium vulgare
Mint Family (Lamiaceae)

Description: An erect plant, 8–24", with a square, hairy stem. The leaves are simple, opposite, oblong or ovate, ¾–1½" long, with a smooth margin. The flowers are found in dense terminal and axial clusters. The flowers are purple, pink, or white. The tubular corolla is 2 lipped (the upper, 3 lobed; and the lower, 2 lobed), with a hairy calyx and 4 stamens.

Bloom Season: Mid-June–September

Habitat/Range: Woodlands, thickets, and roadsides. Found throughout the region.

Comments: The leaves are often dried and used as a seasoning.

GROUND IVY
Glechoma hederacea
Mint Family (Laminaceae)

Description: Small, creeping plants, 4–12" long, with square stems. The leaves are simple, opposite, round to kidney shaped, and ½–1" long, with a scalloped margin. Several flowers are found in whorls in the leaf axils. The flowers are ½–¾" long and blue-violet. The tubular corolla is 2 lipped. The upper lip is 2 lobed, and the lower lip is 3 lobed. The 4 stamens are not protruding.

Bloom Season: March–early July.

Habitat/Range: Moist woodlands, thickets, roadsides, and disturbed areas. Found throughout the region.

Comments: Naturalized from Eurasia. Once established, this plant can spread rapidly by rooting at the nodes and can form a dense ground cover that makes it difficult for other species to establish themselves. Damaged foliage has a strong mintlike odor. Known to be toxic to horses and possibly to humans. A leaf tea was used traditionally in folk medicine for the treatment of lung and kidney ailments.

HENBIT
Lamium amplexicaule
Mint Family (Lamiaceae)

Description: A square-stemmed plant, 2–15" long, often arching and hairy or hairless and branching at the base. The leaves are opposite, kidney shaped to round, and up to ½" wide. They are prominently veined, with a notched base and a toothed or lobed margin. The upper leaves are sessile while the lower leaves are stalked. The lavender-colored flowers are found in whorled clusters of 5–10 in the axils of the upper leaves. Individual flowers are sessile and ¼–¾" long, with a hairy, 2-lipped corolla and protruding stamens.

Bloom Season: March–June.

Habitat/Range: Fields, roadsides, and waste areas. Found throughout the region.

Comments: This European introduction has been proven poisonous to livestock, particularly sheep.

PEPPERMINT
Mentha aquatica X *spicata*
Mint Family (Lamiaceae)

Description: Plants are 1–3' tall with a square, purplish-tinged stem. The leaves are simple, opposite, 1–3" long, narrowly ovate to lanceolate, and stalked, with a toothed margin. Numerous pale lavender flowers are found in clusters encircling the 1–4" long terminal spikes. Individual flowers are about ¼" long and tube shaped, with 4 lobes and stamens that are protruding from the corolla.

Bloom Season: August–September.

Habitat/Range: Along streams and moist places. Found scattered throughout the region.

Comments: This European introduction is believed to be a hybrid between Spearmint (*M. spicata*) and Water Mint (*M. aquatica*). English colonists introduced the plant into North America. They planted Peppermint for use as a flavoring and also as a folk remedy for a variety of ailments, including stomachaches, diarrhea, colds, and cramps.

BERGAMOT
Monarda fistulosa
Mint Family (Lamiaceae)

Description: An erect, square-stemmed plant, reaching 2–4' in height, with gray-green foliage. The simple leaves are opposite, lanceolate to narrowly ovate, and 2–3" long, with a pointed tip and smooth margin. The pink to lavender flowers are on crowded terminal heads that are 1–1¾" wide. Individual flowers have 2 elongated lips and can reach up to 1" in length. The upper lip is 2 lobed, and the lower lip is 3 lobed. Two stamens are present. Each flower head is composed of 20–50 individual flowers. Each blooms separately and is pollinated by insects, like butterflies, with long tongues. Beneath the flower heads are pale green bracts that are leaflike and often tinged with pink.

Bloom Season: Mid-July–August.

Habitat/Range: Woodlands, fields, and thickets. Found throughout the region to central Maine.

Comments: Native Americans used a leaf tea to treat colic, colds, stomachaches, insomnia, and heart-related problems and to reduce fevers. The highly aromatic leaves are used in the making of mint tea. The strong odor associated with the plant is from volatile oils found in specialized, hairlike cells called trichomes.

SELF-HEAL

Prunella vulgaris
Mint Family (Lamiaceae)

Description: Creeping, branched plants, 2–12"
tall, with a square stem. The leaves are simple,
opposite, narrowly ovate, and 1–3" long, with a
smooth or toothed margin. The flowers are
crowded on terminal spikes, ¾–2" tall. The
flowers are purple to white in color and about ½"
long. The corolla is 2 lipped. The upper lip is 3
lobed while the lower is 2 lobed. The 4 stamens
present do not protrude out past the corolla.
Bracts are hairy.

Bloom Season: Late May–early September.

Habitat/Range: Found in fields, roadsides, and
weedy areas throughout the region. Can form
dense colonies because of its ability to root at the
leaf nodes.

Comments: It is believed that Self-Heal is a mix
of native and Eurasian introduced species. Unlike
most members of the Mint Family, this plant has
no characteristic odor that would identify it as
such. The plants were used in Eurasia to treat a
wide range of ailments. The plant derives its
common name from its use during medieval times
to heal the wounds of soldiers. Researchers today
believe that the plant may have some antibiotic
activity. These plants are also rich in antioxidants,
especially rosmarinic acid.

BLUE CURLS

Trichostema dichotomum
Mint Family (Lamiaceae)

Description: These plants are highly branched,
hairy, and 6–30" tall. The leaves are simple,
opposite, oblong to ovate, ½–2½" long, and short
stalked, with a margin that can be smooth, lobed,
or toothed. The blue to purple flowers are found
on panicles. The flowers are up to ¾" long, with a
2-lipped corolla and 4 stamens that are long and
curve out of the flower.

Bloom Season: August–early October.

Habitat/Range: Sandy soils in open woodlands,
fields, and roadsides. Found throughout the range
to southern Maine.

Comments: The blue flowers, long curved
stamens, and style make for easy recognition of
this native species.

TWINFLOWER
Linnaea borealis
Twinflower Family (Linnaceae)

Description: These trailing plants are up to 4" long and hairy stemmed. The light green leaves are simple, opposite, ovate, ½–¾" wide, and short stalked, with a toothed margin. The flowers are found in pairs. They are long stalked, nodding, pink or white, bell shaped, and ½" long, with a corolla that is 5 lobed and hairy inside.

Bloom Season: Mid-May–mid-July.

Habitat/Range: Cool woodlands and bogs. Scattered throughout the region.

Comments: Some Native Americans used a plant tea to treat painful menstruation and reduce fever in children. The plant is somewhat difficult to harvest because of its scarcity.

PURPLE LOOSESTRIFE
Lythrum salicaria
Loosestrife Family (Lythraceae)

Description: These erect, multibranched plants range up to 5' in height and are usually hairless. The leaves are simple, opposite or whorled in groups of 3, narrowly ovate to linear, 1–4" long, and sessile, with a rounded or heart-shaped base and a smooth margin. Numerous flowers are found on terminal spikes, 4–16" tall. Each purple-pink flower is ½–¾" wide with 4–6 petals that have a wrinkled appearance.

Bloom Season: July–August.

Habitat/Range: Swamps, ditches, and various wet places. Found throughout the region.

Comments: Originally from Europe, Purple Loosestrife can be found in Canada and the continental United States with its greatest population densities centered in the northeastern United States. This plant is considered a serious invasive species. It is nothing short of prolific when it comes to seed production. Purple Loosestrife favors disturbed wetland areas and, once established in a given area, it can form dense stands that quickly crowd out and outcompete many native species. It is estimated that in some areas it has replaced as much as 50 percent of the native species. Few native insect species forage on the plant. In Europe it has historically been used as a medicinal herb to treat stomachaches and sore throats. Modern clinical research has shown that plant extracts exhibit some antibiotic activity and an ability to stop bleeding.

LESSER PURPLE-FRINGED ORCHID
Platanthera psycodes
Orchid Family (Orchidaceae)

Description: These orchids are leafy stemmed and 1–3' tall. The lower leaves are elliptic or ovate; the upper leaves are significantly reduced. Numerous flowers are found in terminal racemes. The flowers are lavender to rose-magenta color. An uncommon white-flower form also occurs in the region. Each is ½–¾" long. The lateral petals are oblong and finely toothed. The lip petal broadens toward the tip and is deeply lobed into 3 parts with each lobe fringed. There is also a long, backward-pointing spur.

Bloom Season: July–August.

Habitat/Range: Wet woodlands and meadows. Found scattered throughout the region.

Comments: The Greater-Fringed Orchid (*P. grandiflora*), also found in the region in the same habitats, is similar in appearance to *P. psycodes* but with flowers up to 1" long. Both of these orchids are known to be pollinated by moths.

ALLEGHENY MONKEY FLOWER
Mimulus ringens
Lopseed Family (Phrymaceae)

Description: Square-stemmed plants, 1–3' tall. The leaves are simple, opposite, narrowly ovate to lanceolate, 2–4" long, and sessile, with a toothed margin. A few flowers arise from leaf axils on short stalks. The blue-purple flower is tubular and 2 lipped. The upper lip is 2 lobed, and the lower lip is 3 lobed with 2 large yellow spots.

Bloom Season: Mid-July–August.

Habitat/Range: Wet meadows, marshes, and stream banks. Found throughout the region.

Comments: The common name is derived from the superficial resemblance of the flower to that of a monkey's face.

BLUE TOADFLAX
Nuttallanthus canadensis
Plantain Family (Plantaginaceae)

Description: An erect plant, 4–20" tall. The stem leaves are simple, alternate, linear, and ½–1½" long, with a smooth margin, while the leaves at the base are opposite and smaller. The flowers, several to many, are on racemes. Each is light blue to violet in color, ¼–½" long, tubular, 2 lipped, and long spurred. The upper lip is 2 lobed; and the lower, 3 lobed.

Bloom Season: May–September.

Habitat/Range: Fields, rocky and sandy open sites. Found throughout the region.

Comments: Blue Toadflax can be abundant in its primary habitat.

SPREADING JACOB'S LADDER
Polemonium reptans
Plantain Family (Polemoniaceae)

Description: The plants range from about 6–24" and can be erect or spreading. The leaves are paired, compound, and divided into 5–20 leaflets. Each leaflet is elliptic to ovate, and ¾–1½" long, with a pointed tip and smooth margin. The flowers are found on loose, open panicles. The light bluish purple flowers are bell shaped with 5 spreading lobes and measure ¼–½". The stamens are nonprotruding.

Bloom Season: May–June.

Habitat/Range: Moist, rich woodlands. Scarce. Found scattered throughout the region except in Maine.

Comments: Native Americans used root preparations to treat eczema, piles, and snakebites, help reduce fevers, and induce vomiting.

213

GERMANDER SPEEDWELL
Veronica chamaedrys
Plantain Family (Plantaginaceae)

Description: Plants are creeping or ascending, 4–20" long, and hairy. The leaves are simple, opposite, ovate, ½–1½" long, and sessile, with a coarsely toothed margin. The flowers are on axillary racemes, purple to bluish purple in color, and stalked, with 4 petals, and measure ¼–½".

Bloom Season: May–July.

Habitat/Range: Fields, disturbed areas, and lawns. Found throughout the region with the exception of the eastern parts of Massachusetts and Maine.

Comments: Germander Speedwell is another European introduction.

COMMON SPEEDWELL
Veronica officinalis
Plantain Family (Plantaginaceae)

Description: A creeping plant, 3–10" long, hairy. Stems have ascending tips. The leaves are simple, opposite, narrowly ovate, ½–2", and stalked, with a finely toothed margin. The flowers are found on axillary racemes. Each flower is pale blue-violet, with 4 petals, and measures ⅛–¼".

Bloom Season: May–early July.

Habitat/Range: Open woodlands, dry fields. Found throughout the region.

Comments: Originally from Europe. Folk medicine traditionally used teas made from the roots and leaves to aid in urination and to treat a whole host of ailments including, but not limited to, asthma, coughs, kidney problems, and jaundice.

THYME-LEAVED SPEEDWELL
Veronica serpyllifolia
Plantain Family (Plantaginaceae)

Description: A creeping plant, 4–12" long, with stems that have ascending tips. The leaves are simple, mostly opposite, ovate, ½–1" long, and stalked or not stalked, with or without a toothed margin. The flowers are either pale blue or white with dark blue stripes. The flowers are found on elongated terminal racemes. Individual flowers measure ⅛–¼" and have 4 petals, 3 of which are rounded with the lower 4th one being somewhat more narrow. In addition, there are 2 stamens present.

Bloom Season: May–early July.

Habitat/Range: Open woodlands, meadows, fields, and lawns. Found throughout the region.

Comments: Naturalized from Europe. Native Americans prepared a tea from the leaves to treat coughs.

WILD BLUE PHLOX
Phlox divaricata
Phlox Family (Polemoniaceae)

Description: Plants are 5–20" tall and sticky hairy. The dark green leaves are simple, opposite, elliptic to oblong, 1–2" long, and sessile, with a smooth margin. Flowers are found on loose panicles. Coloration varies from light blue to purple to white. The flowers range from ¾" to 1" wide and have 5 paddle-shaped, united petals.

Bloom Season: May–mid-June.

Habitat/Range: Moist woodlands, swamps, thickets, and fields. Found scattered throughout Connecticut and Vermont.

Comments: Wild Phlox can form rather large colonies due to its ability to root at the nodes.

PICKEREL WEED
Pontederia cordata
Pickerel-Weed Family (Pontederiaceae)

Description: An aquatic plant up to 36" with a thick green stem. The leaves are simple, arrow shaped or ovate, maintained above the waterline, and up to 8" long, with a smooth margin. Numerous flowers are found on 2–6" tall racemes that extend above the waterline. The flower stalk is subtended by a bract that measures up to 2½" wide. The flowers are violet-blue to nearly white and ¼" wide and each lasts only one day. The flower is tubular and has 2 lips, each indented at the base.

Bloom Season: Mid-July–mid-August.

Habitat/Range: Found in shallow waters such as the edges of marshes, ponds, and lakes. Seldom found growing in water over 3' deep. Common throughout the region.

Comments: The seeds and young leaves of Pickerel Weed are edible. The seeds can be eaten raw, cooked, or ground into flour that is suitable for use in baking.

BLUETS

Houstonia caerulea
Madder Family (Rubiaceae)

Description: A small, delicate plant, 3–6" tall, with erect stems, often found growing in clumplike clusters. The basal leaves are opposite, oblong shaped, and up to ½" long, with a smooth margin. The upper leaves are shorter and narrower. The solitary flowers are pale blue to white with a bright golden-yellow center and ¼–½" wide. There are 4 pointed, petal-like lobes and 4 tiny sepals.

Bloom Season: Late April–mid-June.

Habitat/Range: Meadows, fields, thickets, roadsides, and lawns. Commonly found throughout the region with the exception of extreme northern Maine.

Comments: The primary pollinators of Bluets are native bees. Native Americans prepared a leaf tea to help prevent bed-wetting.

DEADLY NIGHTSHADE

Solanum dulcamara
Nightshade Family (Solanaceae)

Description: This climbing, vinelike plant can grow up to 10' long. The leaves are simple, alternate, ovate to heart shaped, 1–3" long, and frequently lobed. The flowers are found in loose clusters of 10–20. The drooping flowers are blue or purple, with a prominent yellow center, and measure ¼–½" long. The corolla has 5 pointed, recurved, petal-like lobes.

Bloom Season: Early June–August.

Habitat/Range: Open woodlands, thickets, and waste areas. Found throughout the region.

Comments: Introduced from Europe. The leaves and unripened fruit of Deadly Nightshade contain high levels of the alkaloid solanine, which can cause a serious case of poisoning if a sufficient quantity is ingested but is not normally fatal. Plant extracts have been used for centuries to treat a variety of common ailments. Probably the most unique and interesting use of the plant in European folklore was for the removal of witchcraft from both people and animals.

BLUE VERVAIN
Verbena hastata
Verbena Family (Verbenaceae)

Description: Plants are erect, branching, and 1–6' tall, with a square stem that is also grooved. The simple leaves are opposite, narrowly ovate, frequently 3 lobed, and 2–7" long, with a toothed margin. Numerous blue-purple flowers are found on terminal spikes. Each tiny flower measures about ⅛" and has a 5-lobed corolla.

Bloom Season: July–early September.

Habitat/Range: Moist fields, swamps, wet meadows, shorelines, and roadsides. Found throughout the region.

Comments: Although revered as a sacred plant of great healing powers by the ancient Greeks, it is considered by many to be no more than a weed today. Native Americans and early physicians used leaf and root teas as a female tonic; to reduce colds, fevers, and stomach cramps; and to treat dysentery.

HOOK-SPURRED VIOLET
Viola adunca
Violet Family (Violaceae)

Description: This tiny, delicate violet grows 1–4" and may or may not be hairy. The leaves are ovate to round, with a leathery texture, and either notched or blunt at the base. The flowers are long stalked. Each flower is ¼–½" wide and violet-blue, with a ¼" spur that has a hooked tip and hairy lateral petals.

Bloom Season: May–early June.

Habitat/Range: Dry woodlands and sandy or rocky soils. Found in northern Massachusetts and throughout Vermont, New Hampshire, and Maine.

Comments: The dried leaves can be used to make a fair-tasting tea.

AMERICAN DOG VIOLET
Violet conspersa
Violet Family (Violaceae)

Description: This member of the Violet Family grows 2–8" and is hairless. The leaves are simple, alternate, stalked, round to heart shaped, and ½–1½", with a rounded tip, notched base, and toothed margin. The flowers are found above the leaves supported on slender stalks. Each flower averages ¼–½" with a ¼" spur. There are 5 blue-purple petals with fine-line markings on them, hairy lateral petals, and 5 narrow green sepals.

Bloom Season: Mid-May–June.

Habitat/Range: Moist woodlands, meadows, and stream banks. Found throughout the region.

Comments: *V. conspersa* used to be classified as *V. labradorica.*

MARSH BLUE VIOLET
Viola cucullata
Violet Family (Violaceae)

Description: The plants range in size from 5–12". The simple leaves are heart shaped, 1–2" wide, and hairless, with a coarsely toothed margin. The flowers are a lavender color with a dark blue center, ½–1", and stalked above the leaves, with 5 petals, the lateral ones tinged with club-shaped hairs.

Bloom Season: Late April–June.

Habitat/Range: Found in swamps, moist or wet places, bogs, and along stream edges throughout the region.

Comments: Another common blue-flowered violet, *V. papilionacea,* is the state flower of Rhode Island.

WOOD VIOLET
Viola palmata
Violet Family (Violaceae)

Description: Small plants, 4–8". The leaves that appear in spring are heart shaped, 2–6" long, and hairy, with a smooth or lobed margin. Summer leaves are much less hairy and highly dissected. The flowers are stalked above the leaves and average 1–1½" wide. The flowers are pale purple with a white center. The lower 3 petals have a hairy base.

Bloom Season: Mid-May–June.

Habitat/Range: Woodlands and meadows. Found in Connecticut, Rhode Island, Massachusetts, Vermont, and southern New Hampshire.

Comments: This species is threatened in New Hampshire and most probably extirpated in Maine.

BIRD'S-FOOT VIOLET
Viola pedata
Violet Family (Violaceae)

Description: Plants are typically 3–10" tall and smooth. The leaves are compound and divided into 3 leaflets that are highly dissected, with a toothed margin. The flowers are on separate stalks from the leaves. The flowers are blue-violet with a conspicuous orange center in the throat. Each flower measures ¼–1½" in diameter. The 5 petals are beardless. The lower petal is whitish in color.

Bloom Season: May–early June.

Habitat/Range: Open woodlands, rocky ledges, and dry, sandy fields. Found in Connecticut, Rhode Island, and Massachusetts to southern Vermont and southern New Hampshire.

Comments: This native species is the largest flowering violet found in the region.

ARROW-LEAVED VIOLET
Viola sagittata
Violet Family (Violaceae)

Description: A small plant, about 4–8". The simple leaves are arrow or triangle shaped with or without basal lobes, and ½–2" long, with a coarsely toothed margin. The flowers are on long stalks, violet-purple, and ¾–1", with a hairy lower petal that has a white base with purple veins.

Bloom Season: Late May–early July.

Habitat/Range: Open woodlands and meadows. Found throughout the region.

Comments: The Iroquois used this plant as a means of detecting witchcraft.

GREEN, BROWN, AND INCONSPICUOUS FLOWERS

Flower colors in this section range from pale green to brown. The paler hues could grade into white, green, or maroon.

WINGED SUMAC
Rhus copallina
Cashew Family (Anacardiaceae)

Description: A large shrub, Winged Sumac can grow up to 20' tall. It has hairy twigs and a milky sap. The hairy, compound leaves are pinnately divided into 7–25 shiny leaflets. The leaflets are 1–4" long with a prominent winged midrib between each leaflet and a smooth or nearly smooth margin. The small greenish flowers are on dense terminal clusters. Each cluster is pyramid shaped and up to 6" tall. Each flower has 5 petals and 5 sepals.

Bloom Season: July–August.

Habitat/Range: Dry woodlands, clearings, roadsides, and meadows. Found throughout the region.

Comments: Native Americans prepared a tea from the bark to help stimulate milk flow. A root tea was used to treat dysentery, and the berries were often chewed to help reduce mouth sores.

SMOOTH SUMAC
Rhus glabra
Cashew Family (Anacardiaceae)

Description: While this shrub generally grows 5–15', it can reach treelike heights of 30–40'. It has hairless twigs that have a whitish coating and a milky sap. The compound leaves are pinnately divided into numerous leaflets that are narrowly ovate, 3–4" long, and hairy, with a toothed margin. The tiny greenish yellow flowers are found in a large pyramid-shaped terminal cluster that runs 3–12" tall.

Bloom Season: June–July.

Habitat/Range: Grows in dry soils at the edges of meadows, fields, and roadsides. Found throughout the region.

Comments: Native Americans used many parts of this shrub for medicinal purposes. The berries were used as an aid in preventing bed-wetting. Asthma, diarrhea, and dysentery were treated with a leaf tea. A tea made from the roots acted as a diuretic, and a bark tea was used to treat a wide range of ailments from diarrhea to mouth and throat sores.

BLACK SWALLOW-WORT

Cynanchum louiseae
Dogbane Family (Apocynaceae)

Description: This twining vine will grow 3–6' and has dark green foliage. The dark green leaves measure 2–5" long and are simple, opposite, oblong to elliptic, broader at the base, and hairless, with a pointed tip and smooth margin. Three to 10 flowers are found in umbels. Individual flowers measure ¼" in diameter and have a reddish brown to dark purple coloration and a corolla that has 5 triangular lobes and is star shaped.

Bloom Season: Late May–June.

Habitat/Range: Woodlands, meadows, and roadsides. Found throughout Connecticut, Rhode Island, and Massachusetts to southern Vermont, New Hampshire, and Maine.

Comments: Originally introduced from Europe, this invasive species often forms dense stands that can outcompete native species.

JACK-IN-THE-PULPIT
Arisaema triphyllum
Arum Family (Araceae)

Description: The plants range in size from 8–24". There are separate male and female plants with the female plants being larger on average than the male plants. The plants arise from an underground stem (corm) and in any given year may produce either a female or male plant. There are usually 2 long-stalked (8–24") dull green leaves that are divided into 3 leaflets. Each leaflet is lanceolate and has a smooth margin. The flowers are borne on a dense yellow clublike spike (spadix) that is approximately 1–6" tall. The male flowers are yellow and the female flowers are green in color. The spadix is surrounded by a tubular green or purple-striped floral leaf (spathe). The upper end of the spathe is curved over the opening. The flowers are inconspicuous.

Bloom Season: May–June.

Habitat/Range: Rich woodlands, thickets, and swampy areas. Found throughout the region.

Comments: Flies are the primary pollinators of this plant. The bright scarlet fruit is highly conspicuous in late summer and autumn. Native Americans used the plant roots for a variety of medicinal purposes, including treatment of colds and coughs.

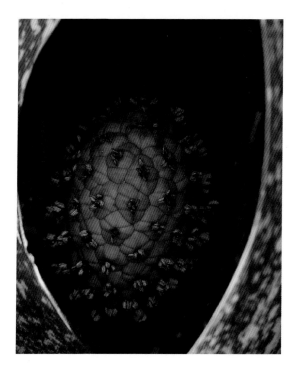

SKUNK CABBAGE
Symplocarpus foetidus
Arum Family (Araceae)

Description: These conspicuous plants reach 1–2' in height. The leaves are simple, basal, and 6–24" long. The dark green leaves are notched at their base and strongly veined. Crushed leaves have a skunklike odor and also contain high levels of calcium oxalate. The leaves are absent at the beginning of flowering. Numerous minute flowers form on a thickened spike (spadix) that is 3–5" tall. The flower stalk is surrounded by a comma-shaped leafy bract (called a spathe) and is purplish brown to green in color.

Bloom Season: February–May.

Habitat/Range: Swamps and moist or wet areas. Common throughout the region with the exception of northern portions of Maine, Vermont, and New Hampshire.

Comments: The spike sprouts in very early spring. The metabolic heat produced from its rapid growth is often sufficient to melt any snow or ice surrounding it. The main pollinators of Skunk Cabbage are flies. They are lured to the plants by the characteristic skunklike odor produced by the volatile chemicals cadaverine and skatole and by the color of the spathe. Both these characteristics help the plant mimic decaying meat, which flies naturally find irresistible. Native Americans utilized the roots and leaves for a variety of medicinal purposes.

WILD GINGER
Asarum canadense
Dutchman's-Pipe Family (Aristolochiaceae)

Description: Plants are 6–12" tall and hairy. The long-stalked leaves are round to heart shaped, hairy, and 3–6" wide. Each leaf has a deep U-shaped notch at its base and smooth margins. A single reddish brown flower grows on or near the ground between the 2 leaf stalks. The flower is somewhat cup shaped and 1–1½" long, with reflexed sepals.

Bloom Season: Late April–May.

Habitat/Range: Rich woodlands. Found throughout the region to southern Maine.

Comments: Wild Ginger was highly valued by Native Americans as a medicinal herb. A root tea was used to treat numerous physical ailments, including, but not limited to, colds, cramps, indigestion, and heart conditions. Due to the root's somewhat peppery taste, it was also used in powdered form as a seasoning by some Native Americans. This native herb is not related to the spice of the same name. *Zingiber offinale,* or Tropical Ginger, is grown commercially in Jamaica and Indonesia and is the source of the spice commonly used today.

COMMON RAGWEED
Ambrosia artemisiifolia
Composite Family (Asteraceae)

Description: A branching plant with a coarsely hairy and erect stem, 1–4' tall. The leaves are pinnately lobed and narrowly ovate or ovate in shape. The lower leaves are opposite with a smooth margin. The upper leaves are alternate with a smooth margin. The flowers are numerous and found in terminal and axial clusters on erect spikes. The male and female flower heads are separate. The male heads are stalked with a yellow-green central disk, while the female flower heads are stalkless with a green central disk.

Bloom Season: August–September.

Habitat/Range: Waste areas, fields, and roadsides. Common throughout the region.

Comments: Common Ragweed, along with Great Ragweed (*Ambrosia trifida*), is the primary cause of hay fever. The flowers do not readily attract insects and are mainly wind pollinated. Some botanists have estimated that during the 2-month-long flowering season, an individual plant is capable of producing upwards to a billion pollen grains, which can be carried by winds for several hundred miles from their source point. Native Americans rubbed the leaves on insect bites. A leaf tea was prepared and used to combat fevers and nausea. Menstrual ailments were treated with a root tea preparation. The seeds can be a major food resource for a number of bird and mammal species.

BLUE COHOSH
Caulophyllum thalictroides
Barberry Family (Berberidaceae)

Description: Erect plants, 10–30" tall. The two leaves are opposite, ovate, 2–3" long, and 2–5 lobed, with a smooth margin. The larger lower leaf is highly divided while the upper leaf is smaller and much less divided. The flowers are found on loose clusters, 1–3" tall. The flower color ranges from a purplish brown to a yellowish green. Each flower has 6 pointed, petal-like sepals and 6 small yellow petals.

Bloom Season: End of April–May.

Habitat/Range: Rich, moist woodlands. Found throughout the region.

Comments: Native Americans used Blue Cohosh extensively. A tea made from the roots was used to treat ailments such as urinary tract infections and abdominal cramping and to aid in labor. Historically, physicians have used root extracts to treat uterine diseases. Plant extracts have been shown to stimulate smooth muscle contraction and to increase blood pressure and were believed able to cause abortions. Colonists also roasted and ground the seeds for use as a coffee substitute.

BURNING BUSH
Euonymus alata
Staff-Tree Family (Celastraceae)

Description: A highly branched shrub, 3–12' tall. The branches are frequently edged with 4 winglike projections that have a soft, corklike texture. The leaves are simple, opposite, narrowly ovate or elliptic, and ½–2" long, with a pointed tip and finely toothed margin. The inconspicuous flowers are usually found lying flat against the leaves and are greenish yellow in color with 4 petals.

Bloom Season: May–early June.

Habitat/Range: Woodlands and disturbed areas. Found throughout the region.

Comments: Introduced from Asia, it has become a popular plant for landscaping. Burning Bush readily naturalizes in woodlands and is extremely shade tolerant. The plant grows rapidly and often forms dense stands that quickly outcompete other native species. The leaves turn an attractive bright red in the fall (hence the common name). The major mechanism for seed dispersal is birds that feed on the reddish purple berries.

CYPRESS SPURGE
Euphorbia cyparissias
Spurge Family (Euphorbiaceae)

Description: Plants are 6–12" tall and contain a milky sap. The dark green leaves are numerous, alternate, linear, ½–3" long. Up to 10 small greenish yellow flowers are found on umbels. The ⅛" wide flower is devoid of petals and has 2 yellow petal-like bracts that turn orange to an orange-red with age. There are separate male and female flowers.

Bloom Season: May–mid-June.

Habitat/Range: Roadsides, weedy and disturbed areas. Found throughout the region.

Comments: This species was introduced into North America from Europe. The plants can spread rapidly from their horizontal root system and form dense colonies. Contact with the plant can cause a serious skin irritation in susceptible individuals.

LEAFY SPURGE
Euphorbia esula
Spurge Family (Euphorbiaceae)

Description: Plants are erect, 6–30" tall, with a tough, woody stem and milky sap. The stems are smooth and usually unbranched. The bluish green leaves are simple, alternate, lanceolate, ½–1½" long, and sessile, with a smooth margin. The leaves are arranged in a spiral-like fashion around the stem. The flowers are on umbels with 7–15 spokes. They are greenish yellow and ⅛" wide and lack both petals and sepals. There are separate male and female flowers.

Bloom Season: May–early July.

Habitat/Range: Roadsides and areas with dry soils. Found in Connecticut, Massachusetts, Rhode Island, and southern Vermont to northern New Hampshire.

Comments: Leafy Spurge originated in western Asia. It can be a serious weed of pastures and even roadsides. Dense growth of the plant displaces many native species thus reducing community biodiversity. In addition, the roots are known to secrete chemicals that alter or deter the growth of other plants. The plant is poisonous to most livestock except for sheep. The plant's milky sap can cause a severe dermatitis in humans.

GROUND-NUT
Apios americana
Bean Family (Fabaceae)

Description: This vinelike plant can be found growing up to 10' long. Leaves are divided into 5–7 ovate leaflets each 1–2½" long and green, with a smooth margin and pointed tip. Leaflets may or may not possess short hairs. The flowers are found in dense racemes arising from leaf axils. Individual flowers are about ½" wide, and brownish purple with a hoodlike appearance. Flowers are also highly fragrant.

Bloom Season: Early August–mid-September.

Habitat/Range: Moist woodlands, meadows, and thickets. Found throughout the region.

Comments: The root tubers were collected by Native Americans and prized as a favorite food. It is believed that these root tubers may well have been instrumental in helping the Pilgrims to survive their first few winters in North America.

FALSE HELLEBORE
Veratrum viride
Bunch-Flower Family (Melanthiaceae)

Description: These erect, nonbranching plants grow between 2 and 6' tall. The leaves are simple, alternate, elliptic to ovate, pleated, and up to 12" long. In addition, they have pointed tips and conspicuous parallel veins, are green-yellow in color, with a smooth margin, and are often found clasping the stem. The flowers are found on panicles that are 6–20" tall. The flowers are star shaped, yellowish green, with 3 petals and 3 sepals, and measure ½–¾" wide.

Bloom Season: Late May–early July.

Habitat/Range: Moist woodlands, swamps, and stream banks. Common throughout the region.

Comments: This native plant is one of the earliest to send up leaves in the spring in the region. The roots and foliage are highly poisonous and potentially fatal if ingested. Small amounts of the plant were originally used to relieve pain and as a sedative for the heart.

BROAD-LEAVED HELLEBORINE
Epipactis helleborine
Orchid Family (Orchidaceae)

Description: This introduced orchid species grows 1–2½' tall. The leaves are simple and lanceolate, with a smooth margin. Leaves clasp the stem and decrease in size as stem height increases. The flowers are on slender racemes. Individual flowers are ½–¾" wide and pale yellow-green with reddish brown patches. Sepals and petals are narrowly ovate with pointed tips. The lip petal is cup shaped.

Bloom Season: July–August.

Habitat/Range: Roadsides and woodlands. Found throughout the region.

Comments: This naturalized orchid was first introduced into North America from Europe in the late 1800s. Several color forms exist. The white (*E. helleborine* forma *alba*), yellow (*E. helleborine* forma *luteola*), and variegated (*E. helleborine* forma *variegata*) forms are extremely rare. The green form (*E. helleborine* forma *viridens*) is the most common of the color variants.

LARGE PAD-LEAVED ORCHID
Platanthera macrophylla
Orchid Family (Orchidaceae)

Description: This member of the Orchid Family grows 12–30" tall and sports 2 basal leaves. The glossy-green leaves are simple, nearly round, and up to 6" in diameter, with a smooth margin. Several to many greenish white flowers are found on a terminal cluster. Each flower measures ¾–1" long with 6 petal-like structures. The lip petal has a down-turned spur measuring 1¹⁄₁₀–1¾" long.

Bloom Season: Late June–early August.

Habitat/Range: Found in rich woodlands with little or no understory growth present. The species is scattered throughout most of the region but absent in Connecticut.

Comments: Several similar-appearing species can be found in the region. *P. orbiculata* has a lip spur that measures ½–1¹⁄₁₀" long. The spur length, according to some experts, is the only reliable character difference between the two species. The more rare *P. hookeri* (Hooker's Orchid) has bright green flowers and an upturned lip spur.

BEECHDROPS
Epifagus virginiana
Broom-Rape Family (Orobanchaceae)

Description: A yellowish brown plant with a branching stem, 6–20" tall. The leaves are reduced and scalelike structures about ⅛" long. The flowers are on terminal racemes. The flowers are yellowish white with brown stripes, tubular in shape, with 4 lobes. The upper flowers are larger, up to ½", and male. The lower flowers are smaller, about ¼", and female.

Bloom Season: Late August–early October.

Habitat/Range: Parasitic on the roots of beech trees. Found throughout the region.

Comments: A tea made from the freshly collected whole plant was used in folk medicine to treat diarrhea, dysentery, and cancer. Another common name for this plant was Cancer-Root.

CURLY DOCK
Rumex crispus
Smartweed Family (Polygonaceae)

Description: Plants are 2–4' with an erect stem. The stalked leaves are simple, lanceolate, and 2–8" long, with a pointed tip and a very distinct wavy margin. The lower leaves are longer and more rounded than the stem leaves. Numerous tiny (⅛") flowers are on spikelike racemes. The flowers start out greenish red in color then turn brown at maturity.

Bloom Season: Late May–early July.

Habitat/Range: Weedy areas, meadows, and roadsides. Found throughout the region.

Comments: This species was introduced from Europe. A tea made from the roots was used in folk medicine to treat a variety of ailments. Often categorized as a pest species in croplands and pastures. Found to be toxic to poultry. The seeds, however, are considered to be an important food source for sparrows and finches.

INDIAN CUCUMBER ROOT
Medeola virginiana
Ruscus Family (Ruscaceae)

Description: These erect nonbranching plants are 6–30" tall. The young plants have a slightly woolly appearance to them that is usually lost with age. The leaves are found in either 1 or 2 whorls. The plants that display only 1 whorl of leaves don't flower. The leaves are simple and lanceolate to narrowly ovate and measure 2–6" in length. In addition, the green leaves have pointed tips and a smooth margin. The flowers, usually 3–9, are found on umbels. Each greenish yellow flower measures up to ½" wide and has 3 petal-like sepals, 3 recurved petals, and 3 long, brown stigmas that are also recurved.

Bloom Season: Late May–early July.

Habitat/Range: Rich woodlands. Found throughout the region.

Comments: This native plant has a root that is edible. The root has the smell and mild taste of cucumber. Native Americans used this plant as a foodstuff. It has become scarce in some locales due to overcollecting.

SMOOTH SOLOMON'S SEAL

Polygonatum biflorum
Ruscus Family (Ruscaceae)

Description: Plants are arching or erect, 1–3' long. The leaves are simple, alternate, broadly lanceolate to narrowly ovate, and 2–5" long with smooth margins and conspicuous parallel veins. The leaves and stem are hairless. The yellowish green flowers are found in the axils, usually as singles or in pairs. Occasionally found in a cluster of 3–4. Individual flowers are up to ½" long, bell shaped, drooping, and 6 lobed.

Bloom Season: Mid-May–early June.

Habitat/Range: Thickets and moist or dry woodlands. Found in Connecticut, Rhode Island, and Massachusetts to southern New Hampshire and southern Vermont.

Comments: Scientists no longer recognize Great Solomon's Seal (*P. commutatum*) as a separate species but rather as a subspecies of *P. biflorum* and have renamed it *P. biflorum commutatum*. The roots of Smooth Solomon's Seal were used by Native Americans to prepare a tea for the treatment of lung ailments and as a surface wash for cuts and bruises.

GOLDEN SAXIFRAGE
Chrysosplenium americanum
Saxifrage Family (Saxifragaceae)

Description: These small plants grow 2–8" and are highly branched. The leaves are ovate to round and up to ½" wide, with a smooth margin. The lower leaves are opposite and short stalked. The upper leaves are alternate and short stalked. The flowers are solitary and found at the end of branches. Petals are absent. Flowers have prominent orange anthers.

Bloom Season: Late April–May.

Habitat/Range: Wet woodlands and muddy soils. Found throughout the region.

Comments: The tiny flowers are pollinated predominantly by beetles and flies.

BUR-REED
Sparganium americanum
Bur-Reed Family (Sparganiaceae)

Description: An aquatic plant, grasslike in appearance, with a partially submerged zigzag-shaped stem. The leaves are flat, 2–3" wide, 24–36" long, and usually partly submerged, with a smooth margin. The sepals and petals of the flowers are reduced to scales. The flower heads containing numerous small green flowers are found on a stout stalk. The female flowers are about 1" in diameter and possess a single stigma. Above the female flower heads are, usually, 5–8 smaller male flowers. The male flowers quickly wilt away after pollination has ended.

Bloom Season: August–early September.

Habitat/Range: Shallow waters and muddy soils. Found throughout the region.

Comments: This native species is often found in dense stands along the water's edge. The seeds are eaten by a variety of waterfowl.

NARROW-LEAVED CATTAIL
Typha angustifolia
Cattail Family (Typhaceae)

Description: Erect plants, 3–8' tall. The basal leaves measure up to ⅜" wide and are very long, lanceolate, and flat, with a smooth margin. The base of this plant is more cylindrical in shape than that of *T. latifolia*. The flowers are on dense spikes. The male flowers are above the female flowers, and there is a gap between them on the spike. As with Common Cattail, the male flowers drop off of the spike shortly after pollen has been shed and hairlike bristles replace the petals and sepals.

Bloom Season: June–mid-July.

Habitat/Range: Commonly found in marshes and ditches and on shorelines throughout the region.

Comments: There is still some uncertainty as to whether this species is native or introduced from Europe. Traditional folk medicine used a root tea to treat kidney stones.

COMMON CATTAIL
Typha latifolia
Cattail Family (Typhaceae)

Description: Plants are erect, 3–10' in height, with sturdy stems. The basal leaves are linear, about 1" wide and 3–8' long, flat, swordlike, and light green, with a smooth margin. The base of the plant is fan shaped. The flowers are borne on a dense spike. The male flowers are above the female flowers with no separation between them on the spike. The male flowers fall off the spike after pollen has been shed. Sepals and petals are absent and replaced by hairlike bristles.

Bloom Season: June–mid-July.

Habitat/Range: Commonly found in marshes and ditches and on shorelines throughout the region.

Comments: This native plant spreads by a creeping root system. The plant often forms dense stands in shallow-water environments. The plant generally does not flower until its second year. Botanists estimate that each flower spike can produce 200,000 or more seeds. The roots are high in starch and were eaten by Native Americans and the early settlers like potatoes or ground into flour for baking. Even the young shoots and pollen spikes are edible. Researchers have determined that cattails, from a nutritional standpoint, are equivalent to rice and corn. Native Americans used the roots and seeds to treat burns and wounds and to combat diarrhea. Numerous wetland bird species use cattails for nesting material and cover.

FALSE NETTLE
Boehmeria cylindrical
Nettle Family (Urticaceae)

Description: Erect plants, 1–3' high and hairless. The leaves are simple, opposite, ovate, and long stalked, with a pointed tip and toothed margin. The tiny (1/16") greenish flowers are on spikes that rise from the upper axils. The female flowers are on continuous spikes while the male flowers are found on interrupted spikes.

Bloom Season: July–September.

Habitat/Range: Moist or wet, shady areas. Found throughout the region.

Comments: Although a member of the Nettle Family, this species is devoid of stinging hairs.

WOOD NETTLE
Laportea canadensis
Nettle Family (Urticaceae)

Description: An unassuming woodland plant covered with stinging hairs. The leaves are simple, alternate, ovate, 3–8" long, pointed at the tip, long stalked, and hairy, with a toothed margin. The greenish flowers are about ⅛" wide and lack petals. The male flowers are in panicles that originate in the lower axils. Female flowers are found in loose panicles originating in the upper axils.

Bloom Season: July–September.

Habitat/Range: Rich, moist woodlands and along streams. Common throughout the region.

Comments: This is the only nettle species exhibiting alternate leaf growth.

CLEARWEED
Pilea pumila
Nettle Family (Urticaceae)

Description: These plants are hairless, have a succulent translucent stem, and grow 6–30" tall. The simple leaves are opposite, ovate, 1–6" long, and pointed at the tip, with a rounded base and coarsely toothed margin. They are long stalked, hairless, and conspicuously veined. Numerous greenish white flowers are found on short terminal panicles in axils. Each flower is less than ⅛" with 4 sepals. Petals are absent.

Bloom Season: July–September.

Habitat/Range: Shaded, moist woodlands and along streams. Found throughout the region.

Comments: Often found in dense colonies in its preferred habitat.

GRASSES, SEDGES, AND RUSHES

This section includes examples of some of the more common and important grasses, sedges, and rushes found in New England.

FRINGED SEDGE
Carex crinita
Sedge Family (Cyperaceae)

Description: These green leafy plants are erect or arching, 1–4', with a sturdy triangular stem. There are 3–5 densely flowered spikes each measuring up to 6" long. The spikes containing the female inflorescence are bristly and drooping. A single and much thinner male inflorescence is also present, located above the female spikes. The spikes change from green to brown as they age.

Bloom Season: Mid-May–June.

Habitat/Range: This sedge species is generally found in wet areas such as swamps and pond edges. Commonly found throughout the region.

Comments: This is a native sedge species and one of the most common encountered in the region.

NORTHERN LONG SEDGE
Carex folliculata
Sedge Family (Cyperaceae)

Description: Most often found growing in clumps, these plants range from 1–3' tall with a very thin triangular stem and yellow-green leaf blades. There are 2–4 female spikes and a single male spike. The yellowish green female spikes are somewhat round to egg shaped, up to 1¼" long, and rather weakly inflated. Each spike is well separated on the stem. The lowest spike is on an elongated stalk and is drooping. At the top of the stem sits the slightly elongated male spike, which is tan in color.

Bloom Season: Late May–early July.

Habitat/Range: A variety of wet soil habitats. Commonly found in Connecticut, Rhode Island, Massachusetts, and New Hampshire. Much less frequently encountered in Vermont and Maine.

Comments: *C. folliculata* is a native sedge species.

GREATER BLADDER SEDGE
Carex intumescens
Sedge Family (Cyperaceae)

Description: This is an upright triangle-stemmed plant that grows 1–2½' tall with dark green leaves. There are 2 female spikes each about 1" in diameter and composed of shiny inflated sacs. Leafy bracts are found beneath the inflorescence. The male inflorescence is a much thinner spike.

Bloom Season: Late May–August.

Habitat/Range: Thrives in a variety of wet soils such as swamps and pastures. Commonly found throughout the region.

Comments: A native sedge species usually found growing in clumps.

SALLOW SEDGE
Carex lurida
Sedge Family (Cyperaceae)

Description: Upright plants, 6–30", with a nonbranching, triangular stem. The lower half of each stem has 1–3 yellow-green leaves each up to 12" long and ¼" wide. There are 1–4 female spikes. Each spike is oblong, about 1–1½" long, yellowish green, and composed of numerous slightly inflated flower sacs. The single male flower spike is thin and tan colored. Located below each female spike is a leafy bract.

Bloom Season: May–June.

Habitat/Range: Generally found growing in clumps in a variety of wet habitats (especially wet meadows) throughout the region.

Comments: A native sedge species. It has fibrous roots and rhizomes and can often be found forming clumps. The seeds are an important food resource for waterfowl and other birds.

TUSSOCK SEDGE
Carex stricta
Sedge Family (Cyperaceae)

Description: Plants with a triangular stem, 1–4' tall, growing in tussocks (dense clumps). The leaves are green, linear, and significantly shorter than the fertile spikes. The male flower clusters are a bit shaggy in appearance and have a tan coloration. The color of the female clusters tends to be more reddish brown or purplish brown. The female clusters are narrow and composed of numerous small, flattened sacs and are situated below the male spikelets. There is a total of 2–4 spikelets on each plant with each averaging about 1½" long.

Bloom Season: May–July.

Habitat/Range: Found in a variety of wet environments, especially in swamps and marshes and on shorelines. Commonly found throughout the region.

Comments: This native sedge is the most common swamp sedge in New England and has a very distinctive appearance, making it easily recognizable in its habitat.

BLISTER SEDGE

Carex vesicaria
Sedge Family (Cyperaceae)

Description: Plants are up to 2½' long with blue-green to light green leaves and a slender, reclining stem. There are 1–3 green spikelets, each approximately 2½" long by ¾" wide.

Bloom Season: Mid-May–June.

Habitat/Range: Often found growing in large stands in wet meadows, bogs, lakeshores, and marshes throughout the region.

Comments: A native sedge species.

SLENDER CYPERUS

Cyperus filiculmis
Sedge Family (Cyperaceae)

Description: A wiry plant, 4–16" tall, with a triangular stem. There are several leaves that are alternate, medium to dark green, and up to 14" long. Located at the top of the stem is a round, green-colored inflorescence that is sometimes branched. At the base of the inflorescence are 3 curly and shriveled-looking bracts.

Bloom Season: July–August.

Habitat/Range: Often found growing in tufts in sandy soils in dry fields. Not often encountered in the region. Found in Connecticut, Rhode Island, Massachusetts, and southern New Hampshire.

Comments: A native sedge species.

UMBRELLA SEDGE
Cyperus strigosus
Sedge Family (Cyperaceae)

Description: Plants are triangle stemmed, stout, up to 3' tall, and branching at the top. A few short green leaves are found on the lower portion of the stem. Inflorescence consists of an umbel or a compound umbel. Spikelets are ¼–1" long, flat, straw-colored clusters. Their growth pattern is perpendicular to that of the branch, giving each spike a bottlebrush appearance. Three to 8 green bracts, which are leaflike, grow under the branch point.

Bloom Season: July–August.

Habitat/Range: Common in moist or wet areas such as shorelines and meadows. Found throughout the region.

Comments: This is a native species that can develop extensive colonies from spreading rhizomes.

THREE-WAY SEDGE

Dulichium arundinaceum
Sedge Family (Cyperaceae)

Description: A leafy plant, 6–24", with a hollow stem that is more round, unlike the typical triangle stem characteristic of the Sedge Family. The leaves are found along the entire length of the stem, growing in 3 distinct rows. Flat clusters of spikelets arise from the leaf axils.

Bloom Season: Late July–September.

Habitat/Range: Found in a number of wet places throughout the region.

Comments: A native sedge that often forms large, dense colonies by means of spreading rhizomes.

COTTON GRASS

Eriophorum virginicum
Sedge Family (Cyperaceae)

Description: Cotton Grass grows up to 3' tall and has a rather leafy stem. The plants grow from long creeping rhizomes and commonly form tussocks. The leaves are flat and grasslike. The flower heads are on dense terminal clusters that give them a fluffy appearance. They are white to brownish white in color.

Bloom Season: Mid-July–September.

Habitat/Range: Bogs, peaty areas, conifer swamps, and marshes. Found throughout the region.

Comments: This native species is the most common cotton grass found in New England and the tussocks formed can be extremely long-lived. Another similar-looking species, *E. augustifolium*, can also be found growing in the region in the same types of environments as *E. virginicum*.

CHAIRMAKER'S RUSH
Scirpus americanus
Sedge Family (Cyperaceae)

Description: These plants reach 2–4' in height. The stem is strongly triangular with 1 flat side and 2 concave sides. The top end of the stem is pointed. Spikelets are unstalked and composed of tightly clustered, scaly, brown, egg-shaped flowers that grow out of the side of the stem near the top. The clusters of flowers are stalkless. Bracts are absent.

Bloom Season: July–August.

Habitat/Range: Occurs in freshwater as well as brackish waters. Found in southern New England.

Comments: Despite the common name, this native species is a member of the Sedge Family.

DARK GREEN BULRUSH
Scirpus atrovirens
Sedge Family (Cyperaceae)

Description: This member of the sedge family grows up to 4' tall and has a slender, non-branching, triangular stem. The inflorescence possesses relatively few branches, and those present occur at the top of the stem. Compound umbels are found at the ends of the branches. Each cluster contains 6 or more oblong spikelets. Three or more leafy bracts can be found under each umbel.

Bloom Season: Late May–June.

Habitat/Range: Swamps and other wet habitats. Found throughout the region.

Comments: Commonly encountered native sedge species. Bulrushes are members of the Sedge Family *(Cyperaceae)* and not the Rush Family *(Juncaceae)* as the common name would imply. The seeds are eaten by numerous species of birds.

WOOL GRASS

Scirpus cyperinus
Sedge Family (Cyperaceae)

Description: An erect plant, 2–6' tall, with rough-edged leaf blades up to 3' long and a somewhat triangular to round stem topped off with a large and rather shaggy-appearing, slightly drooping inflorescence that is brown in color. Often found growing in clumps. The flower stalks radiate out from a single point on the top of the stem and then radiate out again. Long, leafy green bracts are found at the base of the inflorescence. The spikelets are located on the second set of branches. Each is ¼", oblong to egg shaped, brown to rust colored, and woolly in appearance.

Bloom Season: August–early October.

Habitat/Range: Wet meadows and swamps throughout the region.

Comments: A native species that plays a very important role for wildlife in wetland areas. The tubers and seeds are an important food source especially for birds. The plant has the ability to form dense stands, making it an attractive nesting habitat for a number of bird species.

CANADA RUSH

Juncus canadensis
Rush Family (Juncaceae)

Description: A stiff, erect plant, 1–3' in height, with a rounded stem. The leaves are elongated, round, and marked with faint horizontal rings. The small red-brown flower heads are always found in dense clusters on numerous forking branches. The bracts found beneath the inflorescence are characteristically shorter than the flower heads.

Bloom Season: September–October.

Habitat/Range: Found in a variety of wet habitats throughout the region.

Comments: A commonly encountered native rush species.

SOFT RUSH
Juncus effusus
Rush Family (Juncaceae)

Description: This plant ranges from 1–4' in height, has a soft, rounded, nonbranched green stem, is devoid of leaves, and grows in clumps. A dark-colored basal sheath, 2–3" long, can be found at the base of each stem. The inflorescence originates from a single point from the side of the stem and usually occurs at about midpoint on the stem. A single flower is borne at the end of each branch in the cluster.

Bloom Season: Late June–August.

Habitat/Range: Very common in a variety of wet environments throughout the region.

Comments: One of the most common native species in the region and a strict wetlands species. The tall, dense colonies provide excellent cover and nesting habitat for a number of wetland bird species.

BIG BLUESTEM
Andropogon gerardi
Grass Family (Poaceae)

Description: Plants erect, usually branched, 4–8' tall, with a leafy stem blue-green in color and possessing several alternate dark green leaves. Radiating out from the top of the stem are the flower branches. The 3–4" long branches take on a rather coarse, fuzzy appearance and are purplish to bronze colored.

Bloom Season: August–September.

Habitat/Range: Grows in fields, along roadsides and shorelines. Found throughout the region.

Comments: Native grass species. This was one of the most abundant grass species before European colonization and agriculture began to spread across the continent. Both bluestems sport stems that are solid and not hollow like most other grass species.

ORCHARD GRASS
Dactylis glomerata
Grass Family (Poaceae)

Description: Plants grow in clumps and are 2–5' with an erect stem that has a few alternate leaves. The leaf blades have somewhat rough edges and are bluish green. The flowers are found on tall panicles with spikelets in irregular clusters at the end of long, stiff branches. The clusters are rough textured. The plant, like most grass species, is dependent on the wind for pollination.

Bloom Season: May–September.

Habitat/Range: Commonly found in fields, roadsides, and waste areas throughout the region. This grass can tolerate various soil types and grows equally well in full sun or shade.

Comments: Originally from Eurasia. The early colonists were responsible for its introduction along with other grasses such as Timothy Grass for use in pasturelands and hay fields.

BOTTLEBRUSH GRASS
Hystrix patula
Grass Family (Poaceae)

Description: An erect, smooth-stemmed species, 2–4' tall. The leaves are 4–10" long, with a rough surface and smooth leaf sheaths. V-shaped clusters of greenish brown spikelets are found along the stem, imparting a bottlebrush appearance to the plant. Each flower is encased in scales. The scales are tipped with long slender bristles. There can be considerable variation in the distances between groups of spikelets.

Bloom Season: Late June–August.

Habitat/Range: Found in woodlands throughout the region.

Comments: Native grass species.

255

DEER-TONGUE GRASS
Panicum clandestinum
Grass Family (Poaceae)

Description: Deer-Tongue Grass can grow to 3' and has stiff, clasping leaves with conspicuous parallel veins. The leaf sheaths are covered with rough hairs and strongly pull away from the stem. The inflorescence measures 3–6" tall. Individual flowers are tiny and ovate and located at the end of the branches. The entire inflorescence remains hidden within the upper leaf bases and only emerges after the seed has set. Frequently found growing in large clumps. The leaves can persist through the winter.

Bloom Season: Late May–August.

Habitat/Range: Grows in woodlands and thickets and along the edges of open areas. Found throughout the region.

Comments: Native woodland grass species.

TIMOTHY GRASS
Phleum pratense
Grass Family (Poaceae)

Description: Nonbranched plants, 1–3' high, with a stiff, erect stem and grayish green foliage. The leaves are 4–12" long, dull green in color, flat, narrow, and tapering to a point. The numerous flowers are on a narrow cylindrically shaped spike found at the tip of the stem. The spike has a rough texture and starts off a pale green color progressing to tan as it ages. The anthers are purple in color and highly conspicuous. The flowers are both wind and insect pollinated. Often this grass forms sizable colonies.

Bloom Season: Mid-June–early July.

Habitat/Range: Found in fields and meadows and along roadsides. Usually requires that the area have nutrient-rich soils. Common throughout the region.

Comments: Introduced by the early colonists for use as a hay plant. The flower spike can produce a significant amount of pollen, making it a common allergen. The grass was named after a farmer who, in the early 1700s, advocated for its use as a nutritious animal feed.

COMMON REED
Phragmites australis
Grass Family (Poaceae)

Description: This thick-stemmed, light green, nonbranching grass can reach a height of 20' and is the tallest nonwoody wetland plant. The blue-green leaves are numerous, alternate, and long (up to 24"), with a flat blade up to 2" wide, a pointed tip, and a rough margin. The upper leaf surface has conspicuous parallel veins. The flowers are found on terminal clusters that are densely branched. The large spikelet starts off reddish in color, then becoming more silvery. As the cluster matures, it takes on a more downy appearance.

Bloom Season: July–September.

Habitat/Range: Found in a number of wet habitats such as freshwater marshes, brackish waters, and waste areas throughout the region.

Comments: This grass spreads mainly by means of rhizomes. Although it produces a large inflorescence, viable seeds are rarely produced. Its rapid growth and ability to form large colonies allow it to easily outcompete other native species, thus reducing plant and animal diversity. It continues to spread through New England at an ever-increasing rate. Botanists have determined that there are at least 20 genetically distinct strains. Of these roughly half are considered to be native species. These native strains are believed to be widely scattered and existing at very low population densities and are less aggressive in their growth characteristics as compared to the nonnative varieties.

LITTLE BLUESTEM
Schizachyrium scoparium
Grass Family (Poaceae)

Description: A leafy-stemmed plant growing 2–4' tall. The leaves are found mainly along the lower half of the plant. The plants are dark blue-green in early summer, rapidly changing to an orange-tan. The dried stems persist through the winter and maintain their orange-tan coloration. The spikelets are found in terminal clusters that can reach up to 2½" in length and are mixed in with the leaves on the stem. Individual spikelets are about ⅜", with long slender bristles.

Bloom Season: Mid-July–September.

Habitat/Range: Old fields, open dry areas, and open woodlands. Common throughout the region.

Comments: This native grass is an important prairie grass species. In this region it can be a prime forage grass, and the seeds are a valued food source for numerous bird species.

BRISTLY FOXTAIL
Setaria faberii
Grass Family (Poaceae)

Description: A leafy-stemmed, branching, 3–6' tall plant. The inflorescence is cylindrical in shape, drooping, and covered with numerous fine hairs. This species is a prolific seed producer. Leaf blades are light green in color, alternate, up to 16" long, linear, and drooping, with scattered rough hairs on their upper surface.

Bloom Season: July–August.

Habitat/Range: Fields, roadsides, and various types of waste areas. Found throughout the region.

Comments: Introduced from China at the beginning of the 20th century. The seeds are a valuable food resource for birds.

GLOSSARY

alkaloid: any of a large group of complex, nitrogen-containing plant metabolites (usually alkaline in nature) that can react with other acidic molecules resulting in the formation of soluble salts. Many alkaloids, when ingested, can affect human physiology to varying degrees including severe toxicity that can result in death.

alternate leaves: leaves that are arranged singly along the stem.

anther: the pollen-producing part of a stamen; has a saclike structure.

anthocyanins: water-soluble flavonoid pigments that are localized in plant vacuoles; responsible for many of the blue, red, and purple colors found in various plant parts.

anthoxanthin: a type of flavonoid mainly responsible for production of a cream or yellow plant pigment.

axil: the angle defined by the upper surface of a leaf and the stem from which that leaf grows.

axillary: produced or arising from an axil.

banner: in reference to the Pea Family, the broad upper petal.

basal leaves: leaves that originate from the base of the plant at ground level.

bearded: of or about structures that bear a tuft of hairs that can be stiff and/or long.

berry: a fleshy fruit that has developed from a single ovary and contains from 1 to many seeds.

betalains: water-soluble chromogenic alkaloids found only in some families belonging to the order Caryophyllales and in a few higher fungi; localized in the vacuoles and responsible for the production of colors ranging from yellow to red-violet.

bract: a specially modified leaf structure generally situated below a flower or flower cluster; usually smaller than the foliage leaves.

bristles: stiff hairs, long or short, erect or curving.

bulb: an underground stem, short and thick, where food is stored.

bulblet: a tiny bulb that is usually found in a leaf axil.

bur: a fruit structure that is covered in either prickles or spines.

calyx: a collective term for the sepals of a flower.

carnivorous: in reference to plants, the ability to break down animal tissues (usually those of insects) and to obtain at least some nutritional benefit from this action.

carotenoids: plant pigments located in the chloroplasts or other plastids that produce yellow, orange, or red coloration in plants, function as accessory pigments in photosynthesis, and aid in protection against harmful ultraviolet light.

catkin: a scaly spike of tiny, unisexual flowers lacking petals.

chlorophyll: the magnesium-containing green pigment found in plants that acts to capture light energy in photosynthesis.

clasping leaf: a leaf whose base surrounds or partially surrounds the stem.

clump-forming: usually of a grass that can grow in small dense clusters that are attached at the base.

compound leaf: a leaf that is divided into 2 or more leaflets.

co-pigmentation: a loose combination of pigments that effect a change in the hue or intensity of a given color.

corm: a thick, vertical underground stem used for food storage.

corolla: a collective term for the petals of a flower.

corona: a crownlike structure in some flowers that is between the corolla and the stamens.

creeper: a trailing shoot that can root at the nodes.

disk flowers: small, tubular flowers that combine with others into a disk shape that makes up the central part of a flower head as is often seen in members of the Composite Family.

dissected (divided) leaf: a leaf exhibiting deep cuts but with the cleft not reaching all the way to the midrib.

erect: having an upright or vertical stance.

escape: a plant that has spread beyond an area, such as a park or garden, where it was deliberately planted.

evergreen: a plant that has the ability to retain its leaves throughout the year.

family: in classification, a grouping of organisms sharing many similar characteristics; closely related genera.

female flower: these are flowers lacking stamens but possessing 1 or more pistils.

filament: the stalk of a stamen.

flavonoid: a water-soluble ornamental plant pigment responsible for blue, red, or purple (anthocyanins) or white to yellow (anthoxanthins) color found in flowers, fruits, seeds, and some leaves.

fruit: the seed-containing part of a plant.

genus (pl. genera): in the classification of organisms, a group of species that share many similar characteristics.

gland: a structure that secretes nectar, oils, or other sticky substances.

head: a crowded cluster of short-stalked or stalkless flowers, sometimes several different types together, that appear to resemble a single flower as is often seen in members of the Composite Family.

hemi-parasitic: partially parasitic.

inflorescence: a flower cluster.

introduced: a plant that has been accidentally or deliberately brought from one region to another and that may or may not naturalize in the new region.

involucre: a bract or a whorl of bracts located beneath a flower or a flower cluster.

keel: a sharp ridge or fold at the back of a leaf sheath or blade; in the Pea Family the term refers to the 2 lowest petals that are joined.

lanceolate: shaped like the head of a lance or spear.

lateral: at the sides.

leaflet: in a compound leaf, one of the bladelike parts.

lip petal: the lower petal of some flowers, such as orchids, that is frequently larger and showier than the other petals.

lobe: part of a leaf or flower that is rounded.

male flower: a flower possessing stamens but lacking pistils.

margin: the edge of a leaf.

midrib (midvein): the central vein of a leaf.

native: refers to the plants that were present in the environment before humans intervened.

naturalized: of or about a plant that has been introduced into a new region either by accident or deliberately and has now established itself in the wild and reproduces on its own as if it were a native species.

nerve: a prominent vein in a leaf.

node: a point on a stem where a leaf or branch emerges.

nodding: downward hanging or bending.

opposite leaves: leaves are found in pairs at the nodes but on opposite sides of the stem.

ovary: the expanded base of the pistil where the ovules and eggs are located; the site of seed development.

ovate: egg-shaped with the widest part near the base, usually referring to a leaf.

palmately compound: leaf with 4 or more leaflets whose midribs radiate out from the same point.

panicle: an open or compact, branching flower cluster in which the main branches are sub-divided; often takes on a pyramidal shape.

parasitic: of or about a plant deriving all its nutrition from another living plant.

pendant: hanging down.

perfoliate leaf: a leaf whose base completely surrounds the stem and appears to be pierced by it.

petal: the brightly colored basic portion of the corolla, usually broad and flat.

photosynthesis: the process by which green plants manufacture simple carbohydrates from carbon dioxide and water using the energy from sunlight, with oxygen and water also as byproducts.

physical (structural) color: the appearance of color caused by a surface structure rather than by pigments.

pinnately compound: of a compound leaf with the leaflets arranged on both sides of the stalk.

pistil: the female organ of a flower; composed of an ovary, style, and stigma.

pollen: dustlike grains produced in the anther of a stamen containing the male reproductive cells.

pollination: the transfer of pollen by any number of physical or biological agents, such as wind, insects, birds, from an anther to a stigma.

prickles: spiny structures on the surface of a plant.

prostrate: lying flat on the ground.

raceme: a nonbranched, often elongated, flower cluster with flower stalks of equal length and attached directly to the main stalk; flowers bloom in a sequential pattern from the bottom upwards.

ray flower: the outer, petal-like flowers found in a composite head.

recurved: curving in a downward or backward fashion.

reflexed: more abruptly bent downward or backward than something that is recurved

rhizome: a horizontal underground stem, frequently enlarged due to food storage; nodes and scalelike leaves may be present.

runner: a stem that is growing at ground level; leaves and roots can develop at the nodes and tip.

sap: general term for the juices of a plant.

saprophyte: a plant that lacks chlorophyll and derives nutrients and energy from dead organic matter.

scale: small, flattened structure such as a highly reduced leaf.

scape: a leafless flower stalk that rises directly from the root.

sepal: a basic part of the calyx, found at the base of a flower; its appearance is petal-like and usually green in color; one of its primary functions is to help protect the flower bud.

sessile: stalkless; attaching directly to the base.

sheath: tubular structure surrounding a part of a plant; in reference to grasses, it is the base of a leaf that surrounds the stem.

shrub: an erect, woody, multibranched plant generally under 20' tall.

simple leaf: a leaf composed of a single blade.

spadix: a dense, fleshy flower spike composed of tiny flowers and usually enclosed in a spathe.

spathe: a large bract or pair of bracts, usually leafy or hooded, that encloses a flower cluster.

species: the smallest unit of classification of living things; a group of similar organisms capable of interbreeding and producing fertile offspring.

specific epithet: the second word of a scientific name.

spike: a simple, elongated, unbranched flower cluster wherein each flower is stalkless or nearly so.

spikelet: in reference to the Grass Family, it is a structure that is composed of overlapping scales that serve to enclose small flowers that lack petals and sepals.

spine: a highly modified leaf or a sharp, often woody outgrowth from a leaf.

spur: referring to flowers, a slender, usually hollow structure projecting out from either the corona or calyx.

stalk: a supporting structure such as a flower or leaf stalk.

stamen: the pollen-producing.male organ of a flower, composed of a filament supporting an anther.

stigma: the tip of the pistil where pollen is received.

stipules: small, leaflike appendages that, when present, are found, usually in pairs, at the base of some leaf stalks.

stolon: a thin, horizontal stem found at or just above ground level that can give rise to new plants at the nodes.

style: the narrow part of the pistil connecting ovary and stigma.

succulent: of the thick and fleshy portions of some plants used for water storage.

taproot: an enlarged, vertical mainroot.

tendril: a slender, twining part of some plant leaves to aid in climbing.

toothed: having sharp, angled projections along the margin of a leaf.

tuber: the fleshy enlarged part of an underground stem that acts as a food-storage organ.

twining: climbing by twisting or wrapping around another object or plant.

umbel: a flower cluster where the individual stalks grow out from the same point; may be simple or compound.

vein: a bundle of vascular tissue that aids in forming the framework of a leaf and is used to transport water and nutrients.

vine: a plant that climbs up and around other plants or objects.

whorled: having a circle of 3 or more flower stalks, branches, or leaves at a single node.

winged: having a thin, flat projection of a stem, seed, or leaf; in the Pea Family the term refers to the 2 lateral petals.

woody: of a plant whose stems are covered in bark.

SELECTED GENERAL READING

Alden, Peter, Brian Cassie, Richard Forster, Richard Keen, Amy Leventer, and Wendy B. Zomlefer. 1998. *National Audubon field guide to New England.* New York: Alfred A. Knopf.

Bessette, Alan E., Arleen Rainis Bessette, William K. Chapman, and Valerie Conley Chapman. 2000. *Wildflowers of Maine, New Hampshire and Vermont.* Syracuse, New York: Syracuse University Press.

Brown, Lauren. 1979. *Grasses: An identification guide.* New York: Houghton Mifflin Company.

Brown, Paul Martin. 1993. *Wild orchids of the northeastern United States: A field guide.* Ithaca, New York: Cornell University Press.

Clemants, Steven, and Carol Gracie. 2006. *Wildflowers in the field and forest: A field guide to the northeastern United States.* New York: Oxford University Press.

Cronon, William. 2003. *Changes in the land: Indians, colonists and the ecology of New England* (20th Anniversary Edition). New York: Hill and Wang.

Foster, Steven, and James A. Duke. 2000. *A field guide to medicinal plants and herbs of eastern and central North America.* New York: Houghton Mifflin Company.

Kaufman, Sylvan R., and Wallace Kaufman. 2007. *Invasive plants: A guide to identification and the impacts and control of common North American species.* Mechanicsburg, Pennsylvania: Stackpole Books.

Kricher, John, and Gordon Morrison. 1988. *A field guide to eastern forests.* New York: Houghton Mifflin Company.

Ladd, Doug. 2001. *North Woods wildflowers.* Helena, Montana: Falcon Publishing, Inc.

Lee, David. 2007. *Nature's palette: The science of plant color.* Chicago: University of Chicago Press.

Marchand, Peter J. 1987. *North Woods: An inside look at the nature of forests in the Northeast.* Boston: Appalachian Mountain Club.

Meyer, Stephen M. 2006. *The end of the wild.* Cambridge, Massachusetts: The MIT Press.

Neiring, William A. 1985. *Audubon Society field guide: Wetlands.* New York: Alfred A. Knopf.

Raymo, Chet, and Maureen E. Raymo. 2001. *Written in stone: A geological history of the northeastern United States.* 2nd edition. Hensonville, New York: Black Dome Press Corp.

Sanders, Jack. 2003. *The secrets of wildflowers*. Guilford, Connecticut: The Globe Pequot Press.

Sutton, Ann, and Myron Sutton. 1986. *Audubon Society field guide: Eastern forests*. New York: Alfred A. Knopf.

Tiner, Ralph W. 1998. *In search of swampland: A wetland sourcebook and field guide*. New Brunswick, New Jersey: Rutgers University Press.

Thompson, Robert. 2005. *Closeup and macro: A photographer's guide*. Cincinnati: F+W Publications, Inc.

Uva, Richard H., Joseph C. Neal, and Joseph M. DiTomaso. 1997. *Weeds of the Northeast*. Ithaca, New York: Cornell University Press.

Williams, Michael. 2006. *Deforesting the earth*. Chicago: University of Chicago Press.

Yahner, Richard H. 2000. *Eastern deciduous forest: Ecology and wildlife conservation*. 2nd edition. Minneapolis: University of Minnesota Press.

INDEX

ABOUT THE AUTHOR

Frank Kaczmarek is a freelance photographer and naturalist. After receiving his master's degree in microbiology, he spent 30 years as a research biologist, having been employed by the U.S. Forest Service, DeKalb Plant Genetics, and Pfizer Pharmaceuticals. He is the co-author of a number of scientific publications.

Photo by Jeff Sims

His nature photographs have appeared in many publications such as *Nature's Best Magazine, Sierra Magazine, National Wildlife, Nature Conservancy,* and *The Plant Cell.*

He lives with his wife, Colleen, a college chemistry instructor, in Oakdale, Connecticut, and they split their free time between Connecticut and Franconia, New Hampshire.